Copyright

UnCloned Marketing

How to Challenge the Norms with Profitable Marketing Campaigns

By

Audria Richmond

Founder and CEO of UnCloned Media, LLC

Ordering Information:

Special discounts are available on quantity purchases by corporations, associations, and others. For details, contact the publisher at the email address below.

Orders by U.S. trade bookstores and wholesalers.

Please contact UnCloned Publishing:

Tel: (901) 238-6859; or visit www.audriarichmond.com

(Hardcover)

ISBN 13: 978-1-7321703-6-0

(Paperback)

ISBN 13: 978-1-7321703-7-7

(E-Book)

ISBN 13: 978-1-7321703-8-4

(Audiobook)

ISBN 13: 978-1-7321703-9-1

(Library of Congress Control Number)

2020905739

Developmental Editing by: Stefanie Manns

Book Cover Design by: Josh Dingle

Interior Book Design by: Audria Richmond

Acknowledgments

It's finally here! My marketing book. I have been in business for 12 years, but I did not get profitable until my five-year mark. For me to write a book to share my struggles when it came to marketing is a testament that things can change in your life if you are willing to learn and do the work.

If I know nothing else, I know that you have to be committed and clear about what you don't like in your life so you can create your dream life. I didn't like the fact that success was so far out of my reach, and that my business was nowhere near what I knew it could be. That's where marketing came in.

I truly believe if I'd never learned marketing, you wouldn't be holding this book in your hands. This book is proof that I mastered something that has allowed me to build a multi six-figure brand. I am so close to becoming a millionaire and I did that in five years.

All because of **MARKETING**.

I am getting emotional as I type this because I remember when I didn't have sh@% . I remember when I could not pay bills and travel to the places that you see on TV. This girl from Orange Mound, Tennessee made it. I may not be a billionaire yet, but I know what it means to not have to suffer or struggle anymore. I know what it means to have a dream and actually profit and have an impact on this world. I want that for you.

I want you to master marketing. I want to give you the tools and knowledge so you can learn in a few hours what took me years to master. You got this.

I am dedicating this book to anyone with a DREAM and VISION! All I ask is that you do the DAMN WORK!

Special Thanks to my entire family and team. You know who you are!

Now let's get to work.

Marketing Toolkit

Before you get started and get ready to fill your bank account, I want to make sure that I have a place for you to continue your learning. Something that I can update on demand. As you can imagine, trying to keep a book updated is challenging, so I have created a **FREE** virtual marketing toolkit that you can access when you visit **www.unclonemymarketing.com.**

Inside this toolkit, you will find additional tools, resources, checklists, and bonus content that didn't make it inside this book. If I would have included it all, this book would be twice the size (LOL). So head over to **www.unclonemymarketing. com** to **#UNCLONE** your marketing with all the exclusive content. Also, tag me on Instagram **@audriarichmond** and use the hashtag **#UnClonedMarketingBook** when you get there.

Remember, it's about taking action!

Table of Contents

TABLE OF CONTENTS

Acknowledgments 4

Marketing Toolkit (Bonus Toolkit) 6

Introduction 11

Chapter 1: The Profitable Power of Trusting Yourself 21

Chapter 2: The Misconceptions of Marketing 31

Chapter 3: UnCloned Marketing: Defined..................................43

Chapter 4: Authority and Credibility 57

Chapter 5: FREE and Paid Offers 79

Chapter 6: Lead Generation Strategy 97

Chapter 7: The Marketing Plan 121

Chapter 8: Launching and Sales 139

Chapter 9: Mastering Your Clients and Customers....................159

Chapter 10: Your UnCloned Marketing

Campaign Success Path Fast Track..167

Conslusion:..187

INTRODUCTION

If you've ever heard me teach or speak, you've probably heard me say that marketing saved my business. That is the truth, the whole truth, and nothing but the truth.

Until I mastered marketing—the art of telling people about what we create and convincing them to buy it—I was broke. *Like broke broke*. Like too broke to pay attention *broke*. And it was a level of constant frustration and letdown that you couldn't possibly imagine, or maybe you can, and that's why you picked up this book.

One of the most frustrating experiences in business is to have a product or service that you've poured your blood, sweat, tears, and money into, but, after all your efforts, you still can't get anyone to buy it. As business owners, we build things for people to buy. We see things. We feel things. We create things. We believe in possibilities. We find problems and create solutions to solve them. That's what we do. That's how we're wired, and that's what makes us who we are. So you know exactly what I mean, exactly how it feels, to live through one flopped launch after the next. I've never been a quitter, but I am damn sure a crier. And I cried for years—a lot. I was on the brink of becoming a statistic—yet another hopeful entrepreneur who couldn't figure out how to turn their dream into enough dollars to survive.

Like you, I've always been a big-picture thinker and creator, so I knew in my soul that my ideas were epic. Whether we were talking photography, fresh juices, or graphic design, I knew I had what it took to be successful. I knew there were people who needed me and what I had to say and sell. Back then, I could get a customer here and there, but nowhere near the amount of people I needed to be consistently profitable. I was full of all these amazing, creative business ideas, but, on most days, my pockets were as empty as Chik-Fil-A on a Sunday.

It would take a few years of continuing to struggle in business before I realized that regardless of how cute and talented I was, there was still something missing. I was doing everything I knew how to do, and still couldn't figure out why potential clients and customers were not beating down my door. Here I was, studying the most successful businesspeople I could find. I bought all of these blueprints and swipe files and scripts from gurus who were supposed to tell me *exactly* what to do to make my business work. And I mimicked everything they did, thinking that if I imitated the best, I could replicate their success.

If you look back at some of my earlier webinars and videos, you'll see someone who was almost unrecognizable in comparison to who I am today and how I show up. If I am being honest, I could have put the C in copycat. I would come on camera, dressed in my pressed, Sunday's Best. (I even had on pearls, okay? *Pearls.* Don't believe me? Go watch.) All I needed was a black briefcase and a pair of thick bifocals, and I could have been selling life insurance to your grandma or teaching Sunday school—there is absolutely nothing wrong with either of those careers by the way; they're just not what I do—instead of teaching you how to build your brand.

I was a clone.

Instead of innovating, I was imitating. Instead of creating, I was copying. I was playing it way too safe.

But that's what we all do, right?

We're taught, in business and in life, that if we show up and do exactly what everyone else does, we'll eventually get to where they are. It's the unspoken rule of success that, until we know better, we all blindly follow, but then wonder why we never reach the top, or, in some instances, even get off the ground.

The problem is that becoming an exact replica of somebody else almost never works. And if you get lucky and it works once, maybe twice, I can promise you will only yield results in the short term. Besides, copying is really smoke and mirrors. It's an illusion that makes us feel safe, when, in actually, it's not safe at all.

Copying is really a crapshoot because we can do what the next person does, down to the letter, and still not get the same result.

Copying is really a copout because we are afraid to deviate from a plan.

Copying is definitely a condition, a disease, that is killing the creativity of small business owners everywhere because we don't realize how dope we really are.

I decided to start betting on myself. I learned that to be profitable, I had to be different. I had to stand out. I had to UnClone.

The moment I decided to start experimenting with my marketing, everything changed. I took the pieces of marketing philosophies and proven methods that worked, but I decided to do things my way. I gave myself permission to start tinkering with stuff, and soon, I was a mad marketing scientist. Sh@% blew up and starting smoking. I flopped. I lost money. I launched to crickets. When that happened, I went back into the lab and tried new things. New formulas. New systems. New ways to prove to my audience that I was the best marketer alive. I built a hell of a personal brand. You can find that foolproof framework in my first book, *Are You Ready for Yes: How to Prep Your Personal Brand for Lucrative Opportunities*. In doing that, I learned how to really market myself and my products and services. And I started attracting clients on demand.

The bolder I got—

The louder I got—

The more creative I got—

The more willing I was to take risks—

The more money I made.

And so the audacious, all-in-your-face Audria that you know, and hopefully love, today was born.

I had to establish myself as the go-to guru in my industry. I had to get more intentional about my marketing. I need to strategize more, and start being my truest self. I had to show up online so much that it made people sick—they call that hating in business. I talked about myself and my expertise more than I ever had before. I stepped up the experience

I wanted to deliver to my clients. I stopped being afraid to think and act differently. All of this is what set me apart from everyone else around me.

But you know what I had to do the most?

I had to shake off my fear of getting it wrong if I didn't do it the way the marketing rules said I should.

And so do you.

Everything that I am going to teach you in this book is based on years of flops and wins, data and lessons learned from launches that worked and some that didn't. I am sharing research and results that I have been able to replicate for myself and my clients over and over and over again. But what I am really sharing with you is a reminder that you are what the world has been waiting for. I am sharing permission for you to become your complete, brilliant, UnCloned self.

This book is tactical, so you will learn a lot. You will get inspiration, insight, and ideas. But what you won't get is heart. What you won't get is genius or a desire to share something in a way that the world has never seen.

Why?

Because all of that is already inside of you.

WHO THIS BOOK IS FOR

This book is for people who have something to sell or an idea for something to sell.

I don't care what you are selling. It could be a product or a service. It could be cat litter, copywriting, or crisis management services. All you need is an offer to market.

I wrote this book for every business owner who has been where I've been. Frustrated. Hopeless. Overwhelmed. Confused. Desperate. Sick and tired of being sick and tired—and not making the money you know you're capable of. Teetering right on the edge of giving up on yourself and your businesses. Think of this book as one of those floaties you put around a kid in the pool. I know you've been drowning trying to figure this marketing thing out. I am here to teach you how to swim.

I get that you started this business to make a name for yourself and to make money. I know that your hopes and dreams are on the line. I know you want to win. And I want you to know that marketing is the missing piece to your profit puzzle. This book is going to help you finally find it.

I, along with hundreds of my students and clients who've put the UnCloned Marketing framework to work, are proof that profitability is possible. Whether you've made no money or you're fresh off your first flopped launch and you're not sure what to do next, you're in the right place.

Now, let's market your way to millions.

HOW TO USE THIS BOOK

There is a difference between a framework and a step-by-step guide. This book is more of the latter. I wrote this book to give you the essential elements of a profitable marketing campaign. If you take the time to read the book, apply the knowledge, and create each of these essentials, you will transform the way you market what you sell.

This book is not intended as a copy-and-paste product. But it is a rinse-and-repeat process that once you master it, you can use again and again for every marketing campaign you'll ever create.

I am going to break down, piece by piece, everything you need to know and do to build your campaign. Take each chapter and each section, read it through, and do take the actions I recommend along the way. What I don't want you to do is feel pressured to follow this thing to a T. Know what works for you. Don't shortcut or skip major steps, but tailor this process for yourself, your customer, and your campaign.

If you know anyone who cooks great food, you know they love a great recipe. Once they've mastered their own meals, a true cooking enthusiast is always looking to add something else to their repertoire. When they find a recipe that excites them, they'll shop for the ingredients as listed, gather them together, and go in the kitchen to create magic. They may use a recipe for inspiration, but once they get in the kitchen, they allow the spirit to take over. After following the recipe to a certain point, they trust their creative gut to make that cake their own.

They may find that the batter needs a little more butter, and the icing would be creamier with just a little more milk added in. The recipe may say three eggs, but the cook knows they like their cake more dense, so they do four. And when that cake comes out of the oven...it's epic.

I want you to think about this book in the same way. Use everything I teach you here as a list of ingredients and a recipe to guide you. You can trust me and my tried-and-true method as a guide to get you profitable, but this is about you and your business. Trust your gut to know what works.

Your marketing is your cake. Bake it how you wanna bake it, baby.

Just make it UnCloned.

CHAPTER ONE
THE PROFITABLE POWER OF TRUSTING YOURSELF

I know this is a book about marketing and not personal development. But to me, it's impossible to talk about one without the other.

Before there is creating an offer, getting clients interested in it, launching, selling, and servicing, there is something that has to come first—**your mindset**.

Above anything else, UnCloned Marketing is about doing something different, something more than people have ever seen. It's about a willingness to be "the first to do it first." UnCloned Marketing is about leading the pack. It's about setting the world on fire. To market yourself and your business in this way, you have to be comfortable with pushing the envelope. You have to take risks. And this, homies, requires a different type of mindset.

It requires a different version of you.

Notice I didn't say a *new* version of you. I believe we all have that bold, fearless, I-couldn't-care-less-what-the-world-thinks version of ourselves. This is the person who wants to shake off expectations and who the world wants them to be. The person who wants to take more chances and constantly try new things. The person who doesn't play it safe at all, and, as brilliant as they are, has only tapped into a fraction of the epicness they are capable of creating. The person who is so freakin' bright that there hasn't been a pair of shades made that can handle all of their shine.

That person is in there—*in you*. You just have to allow them to come out to play.

As you begin to open yourself up and shift your mindset to allow your genius and creativity to truly flow, unleashed and unrestricted, that's when the magic happens. That's when the ideas and innovation come. Followed by the audience, and then the clients and customers. And then the money.

Be the you that you want to be. There is power—and plenty of profits—waiting for you when you do.

YES, YOU SHOULD DO TOO MUCH...AND THEN SOME

If I had a dollar for every time someone told me that I was "doing too much," I'd already be a billionaire. To be honest, when I would hear that years ago, I would immediately start to question myself. Instead of owning my individuality, I doubted who I was, my work, and my ideas. I'd think, *Maybe they're right. Was I really too loud? Too bossy? Too extra?* I held back too much, didn't say enough, and found myself constantly feeling like a ticking, creative time bomb that was ready to explode. I didn't fit in anywhere, and my desire to be me and live out my ideas while still being accepted and liked was slowly killing me.

The truth is, when I think about it, I have always been a bit of an outcast. I was the weird one. The one who thought and lived differently than everybody else I knew. It was rare that I met people who "got" me, or who, honestly, could keep up with the pace at which I wanted to create. For years, I thought there was something wrong with me. Until I realized there was actually something wrong with the world and the small spaces I was stuck in. I was trying to force myself to stay where I did not belong. I was allowing others' opinions of me to put me in a box. So I broke out of it and saved my life and my business.

Now, I speak my whole mind. I create constantly. I push myself. I promote myself relentlessly. You can find me online almost every minute of every day. I live to market my offers and tell the world about who I am and what I do. Whenever I feel like I've reached the pinnacle of success, I search for ways to expand myself. I am constantly reaching, stretching, growing. If people are not saying I am too much, then that means I need to do more. I want my big ideas to be bigger. I want to be seen and remembered. I want to be the first in everything I do.

I am the Queen of Too Much, and I wouldn't want it any other way.

I've spent the last 12 years proudly wearing my crown. I've made a name for myself as an expert, built several success-ful companies, and helped a lot of people to do the same. I worry less and less about criticism or praise. I'll be honest, every once in a while, those voices of doubt and hatera-tion will try to creep in. But I shut them down, remember my crown, and keep it pushing.

I can guarantee you that people will tell you that you are too much too. They will criticize you and talk behind your back. They will unfollow you. They will scroll past the beautiful social media posts you worked so hard on without liking or commenting, and they'll unsubscribe from your list for send-ing too many sales emails. Your success will prick a hater's heart, and it's okay. Let them go.

People will tell you that you are crazy, and your wild ideas will never work. They will tell you that you should just play it safe, stay in your little box, and do it the way it's always been done. And when that happens, which it will, know that's not a sign that you're doing something wrong.

It's actually a sign that you're doing everything right.

So I want you to turn up the heat on their asses, okay?

Remember, you will always be too much for people who are not doing enough.

WHEN IT COMES TO BUSINESS, RISK TAKERS
ARE HISTORY MAKERS

If you think about it, risk always eventually results in reward, especially in business. The risk may not pan out right away or make millions of dollars on the first try. But if given enough time and enough tinkering, something epic is bound to happen.

Our history books are filled with people who kept tinkering with their ideas. They were bold and brave enough to go against the grain, to challenge the norms. History makers are people who don't wait for permission or approval. They accept they will be criticized, questioned, and misunderstood. In fact, they understand it's the cost of being a genius, the price of true power. If someone who is destined to create history has an idea, they move. They always do it anyway, whatever their "it" is. They jump and wait for everyone else to grab a parachute and follow.

The truth is, innovation is what makes the world go around. From electricity to your favorite form of entertainment, without someone who was willing to take a risk, you wouldn't have a laptop to create with or Beyoncé's Lemonade album to dance to.

Innovation is what makes people memorable and legendary. And the beauty is we all can create something the world has never seen. We just have to think, live, and create outside of our box.

The people you admire most are typically those who have broken out of every single box the world has tried to put them in.

If Lizzo had stayed in a box, she may be working in a music store, instead of killing it as a plus-sized, thong-throwing, twerkin', flute-playing singer.

If Rhianna had stayed in a box, she may have stopped her career at performing, and not launched one of the most successful beauty and fashion brands in the world.

If Jamie Foxx had stayed in a box, he may still be a goofy-looking comedian instead of a Grammy-winning singer and Oscar-winning actor.

If Marcus Lemonis was afraid to get loud and real about why businesses really fail, and decide to do something about it, there would be hundreds—maybe more—small businesses sinking instead of sailing their way to millions of dollars in revenue.

Lizzo, Rhianna, Jamie, and Marcus are legends of their time. They create fearlessly and break out of the box, and we all reap the rewards of their risks. You may not wear Fenty foundation or watch Marcus's hit television show, "The Profit," but you know someone who does. But the bigger point is, as a business owner, you too can create something that completely changes an industry. If they can do it, you can too. Millions of people could be holding your thing. Your song, your design, your lipsticks—anything that you want to create and build—has the potential to change the world.

It's time for you to move from admiring to being admired.

You are just as legendary as your favorite celebrity or business icon. You are the big brain behind the business. The creator. The innovator. The genius. Before you define yourself by what you do, define yourself by who you are. YOU ARE UNCLONED. And it's time for you to know it—and own it.

You aren't like anybody else. You were created to make history. And nobody, I mean nobody, has built a box big enough to hold you and all of the creativity inside of you that the world is waiting for.

YOU GOTTA SHAKE SOME S%*T UP!

As kids, one of the first things we learn is manners.

The adults in our lives teach us what to say and when to say it. They tell us what to wear and how to wear it. Where you go to school, where you work, where you live, all of it is "supposed" to be the "right" thing. You were raised to follow, not to lead. To fit in, not to stand out. And whenever we try to deviate from the program, we're punished for it. Our parents and teachers freak completely out whenever we try to think outside the box or for ourselves. Every thought we have is plagued with the fear of saying or doing the wrong thing.

To grownups, there is one thing you can be that would ruin your life. And, surprise, it's not failing math or being bad at basketball.

It's being weird.

So we live our lives trying to abide by the rules. And that is where the box that many of us spend our lives in begins. All of that "Don't do this!" and "No, do that!" messes with your mind. It's a cultural conditioning that you struggle to shake. You don't trust yourself to know what's the right thing to do, even though your creative self is scratching and screaming to get out of that box you've been put in.

Now, listen, there are times when you should mind your manners and do "the right thing."

Unless you are Shrek, you probably can't get away with burping and picking your nose in public.

Unless you live on a nudist colony, you probably should put some pants on before you go out for a steak and lobster dinner or to visit your people.

So I hate to admit this, but, yes, sometimes you have to play by some rules—unless we are talking about your marketing.

We are in a world where, in business, you can say, do, or be whatever you want. You can control your voice and own your own platform. You don't have to be in any box. You don't have to play by any rules here. When it's time to tell your audience about who you are and what you've created, just for them, you can do whatever you want to do. In marketing, the "right" thing is your *thing*.

Do your thing. Be weird. Get creative. Break out of that box.

Shake some s%*t up in your business, your marketing, and while you're at it, in your life.

What's the worst thing that could happen? You live out your dreams? You sell a lot of stuff and make crazy money? You become an UnCloned legend that people talk about all their lives? Is that really that bad?

There is power and profits waiting when you trust yourself to be exactly who you are (or who you want to be) and let the whole damn world know it.

CHAPTER TWO
THE MISCONCEPTIONS
OF MARKETING

Before we really dig into how to build a profitable UnCloned Marketing campaign, let's get clear on what marketing actually is.

Marketing is a really big term, and one that we see thrown around all the time. You picked up this whole book about it, likely because you want to demystify marketing and finally figure out how to master it so you can grow your business. You know marketing is something you have to do as a business owner, but to do it, and especially to do it well, you have to know what marketing is and what it's supposed to do.

There are a lot of misconceptions about what marketing is and what it does. So let me set the record straight:

The number one objective of marketing is to support your client or customer in making a decision to buy your product or service.

Marketing is about education. It informs people, telling them everything they want and need to know about you, your product, your service, and the result they can expect to get when they pay you for it. Marketing takes the guesswork out of the purchase. Nobody wants to have to work to pay you. The less tedious your marketing is, the easier it is for people to spend money with you.

Recently, I decided I wanted to learn more about applying makeup so I could show up fresh to death for my videos without having to hire a professional makeup artist whenever I was inspired to go live. So I started searching the educational rabbit hole that is YouTube and came across a bunch of beauty girls who had great tutorials. Excited to buy all of these lash extensions to try, I got my credit card out and ran to the first website. And that's when my enthusiasm started to fizzle—fast.

The product descriptions were boring as hell. There were no instructional videos to show me how I could play with the products. There wasn't enough information to convince me to buy anything.

Refusing to give up, I went to the next site. And then another one. Finally, I found an entrepreneur who made me proud. I was immediately drawn in. Her lash products had creative names. She'd taken the time to create tutorials so I could see how to apply the lash, which helped me to decide which length and look was best for me. I knew I didn't need everything on her site. But I had a ball just looking through the options. She got my time and my money. It was obvious to me, as a consumer, that she understood her market. She thought about how I would experience her website and presented her products in a way that educated and excited me.

This is what marketing should do. If it doesn't wow, it doesn't win.

Great marketing does give your audience a lot of information to process and think about. But that doesn't mean you can't excite them in the process.

The entire concept around UnCloned Marketing was born because I was bored as hell with marketing, at least with the way it has always been done. When I first started getting serious about business, I studied every book, webinar, course, process, and framework out there on marketing, and I didn't fit in any of them. Traditional marketing lacked creativity. There was no individuality or excitement. There was no one encouraging business owners to break rules, to challenge norms, to be loud, to strive to create something fresh and new.

Yet while the gurus were teaching entrepreneurs how to market with textbooks, theories, and templates, the big, highly successful companies that were making major money were doing it by making major noise. They were innovating, tossing all of that you-gotta-do-this-and-that to the wind. The marketing campaigns that were going viral were the ones that were infused to the max with creativity. They weren't just one-and-done promotions. They were well-thought out, well planned, methodical experiences that made people stop and stare. Legendary, highly profitable marketing campaigns are not basic. They give the people what they least expect, and in turn, those people pay. I wanted that for myself and every other business owner out there, especially small businesses.

As I became determined to master marketing in my own business, and naturally narrowed my niche to work more closely with small business owners, I realized that marketing was where most entrepreneurs were dropping the ball—a lot. There wasn't enough being taught on the topic. Everyone was so focused on getting paid that no one was taking the time to get prepared.

We were approaching marketing as an afterthought, and not devoting the time and attention to it that it needed and deserved. We weren't planning out offers, launches, and campaigns. We were watching someone's end result, one webinar or promotion, and assuming that was all there was to it. We were hustling, instead of hunkering down, researching, mapping out master plans, and executing with precision. When it comes to marketing, most small businesses come up with something, throw it out there, and hope for the best. We show up like first-time fishermen instead of pros.

Since I am in a zone, I'll just keep going with that, so you get exactly what I mean. Follow me for a second. I'll bring it back full circle.

If you ever have a chance to kick it with a professional fisherman, you'll soon see their approach is not a game. While an amateur fisherman will put some trash bait on a hook, throw it in the water, and catch what comes, a pro moves differently. She knows what lake to go to. She chooses the right bait for the exact fish she wants to attract. She's not impatient. She will sit in the sun in one spot all day until she gets those bass. She wants the fish she wants, and she's not going to use cheap bait, cut corners, or rush the process.

Marketing is like fishing. The marketplace is a huge lake, filled with fish. We have to decide if we are going to show up like first-time, amateur fisherman or pros. Amateurs don't care what type of fish, or clients, they catch. Their marketing isn't intentional, effective, or reflective of their individuality and what they really want. So they end up hating their clients and full of frustration from what's not working. Pros, on the other hand, catch the clients and customers they want. They want big fish, and they go hard and get them. Or, they go home.

When you look at your business, what's on the end of your fishing hook? Are you catching the fish you really want? If not, you have to switch up your bait.

When it comes to your marketing campaigns, your hook has to give people something to remember. Marketing is a game where the most outlandish, loudest, craziest, funniest, emotional ideas win.

There is no such thing as too far out there. You want to capture their hearts, get them emotional in some way. If you can make your audience laugh, cry, or clutch their pearls, *you* got them.

Marketing that hooks your people and is well-planned and well thought out is like a money-making machine.

CHOOSE YOUR COMFORT ZONE

Marketing is as much about you as it is your potential clients and customers. We often create with the people in mind, and we should. But first, we need to be clear on our own goals and the results we want. Your desires matter, especially in marketing.

Your marketing should be, first and foremost, what feels right to you. I cannot harp on individuality enough. How do you like to speak? How do you like to show up? Are you an in-your-face salesperson that can approach anybody in their DMs, or do you fear rejection, so you only feel comfortable presenting your offer on livestream where you just show up full of personality for the masses? Consider what makes you comfortable when choosing the route that is best for your business and your marketing.

Marketing shouldn't feel forced. It should challenge you, yes, but it should also feel so natural to you that you don't blink twice when it's time to move. Contrary to what the coaches tell you, sometimes your comfort zone isn't a bad thing. Let your comfort zone give you clues about your organic rhythm and how you like to move. Let it guide the offers you create and how you market and sell them. That's the thing about UnCloned Marketing. There is more than one way to skin this cat. We can get you profitable, and you don't have to do it kicking, screaming, and hating the process.

It's always clear when a business owner is selling something they don't really believe in, they are not passionate about, or they are too afraid to take a risk to market.

This is your business, your marketing, your rules.

Regardless of what the gurus tell you, you get to do what feels good to you.

DON'T REINVENT THE WHEEL (AND OTHER TRASH ADVICE)

Everything that I've talked about in this chapter so far is about what not to do in marketing. "They" say your marketing is all about beating somebody over the head with a promotion. Putting up any ol' whack website. Doing 'ish you don't want to do just because. I'd be willing to bet my next PayPal payment from a client that it's probably all advice that you've heard somewhere.

Well, I am here to tell you that most, if not all, of that is trash.

One of my primary motivators for writing this book was to challenge the traditional marketing rules that we've heard for years. Let's talk about a few more popular ones that are out there and why they don't work.

"You don't need to reinvent the wheel." Or another common BS line, "If it ain't broke, don't fix it." We hear this type of business BS all the time. It is anti-creation, anti-innovation, and, ultimately, anti-profits, which means it's horrible advice for businesses. Ask Blockbuster, cab companies, and even pay phone providers if they'd agree. These are all companies and industries that were wiped off the face of the earth because they stayed status quo. Meanwhile, Netflix, Uber, and cell phone providers were inventing new wheels that changed the game.

To win, you have to innovate. You have to create. You have to introduce people to something fresh and exciting. You have to challenge the old mentors and their old models. Sure, there are some marketing fundamentals that are tried and still true. But you cannot be afraid to try something new. With a little creativity, you could be on the brink of the world's next big thing. So you have to create and create and create some more. You have to put on your thinking cap and dig into what's really broke in your industry so you can fix it.

Hint: Just because people are buying something today, doesn't mean it's meeting all their needs. It's just the only option they have.

Everybody thought getting in the car and driving to a store to rent movies was cool until they could watch them from the couch. It was cool to wait outside in the rain to get in the back of a broke-down taxi until you could use an app to bring a chauffeured car to your front door. It was cool to stand on the corner and wait for a public phone until some-body created one you could put in your pocket.

Don't get caught up on what's working for everybody else. Become the next wheel.

"You don't need to follow the trends." If you've been given this advice, ignore it. As a business owner, you need to know what's happening in the world around you, what's hot and relevant, and how you can bring that energy into your marketing.

Marketing changes a mile a minute, and to be UnCloned, you have to be ahead of the curve. Pop culture, current events, the latest in technology and graphic design—all of these are influences on your marketing and business. Consumers crave innovation. Don't look like a dinosaur out here.

"You don't need all of that stuff." My response to this is simple: Oh yeah, you do.

You'll often hear business coaches and experts say you don't need to spend a lot of money to make money. You may have heard you don't need a website. You don't need graphics. You don't need a full-blown marketing campaign, and a few Instagram posts will be enough. Trash, trash, trash. In online business, you need all the things.

I am a believer in starting with what you have, but I am firm in my belief that you have to spend money to make money.

You cannot show up like a value-menu cheeseburger with fi-let mignon pricing. Everything from your free offer to delivery of your product or service has to be A1. To get the most, you have to be and do the most. Get comfortable with investing in yourself and your business in big ways. If you are not going to go hard, then baby, please go home.

"To win, you have to innovate. You have to create. You have to introduce people to something fresh and exciting."

- Audria Richmond

CHAPTER THREE

UNCLONED MARKETING:
DEFINED

Now that we have a good sense of how to get marketing all wrong, let's get into how to get it *right*. That is where Un-Cloned Marketing comes in.

As you'll learn as you continue reading this book, an Un-Cloned Marketing campaign has a few—okay, I can't lie, a lot—of moving parts. But the core of everything I am teaching you in this book all comes back to one thing—creativity.

I can teach you the technical aspects and tactics for creating a successful launch—in fact, that is what the bulk of this book is about— but as you are learning what steps to take, I want you to always keep at the forefront of your mind that creativity is everything. Disruption is everything. The element of surprise is everything. Sometimes it's about doing it big, big, and other times, it's the little things that stick with people and motivate them to take action. The technical execution of a campaign is one aspect, but the energy and emotion that it stirs in people is something else. That is what memorable and profitable campaigns are really made of.

So with that said, here's the secret sauce. The juice. The must-haves of any UnCloned Marketing Campaign:

It's unpredictable. Think about the last impulse purchase you made. How did the company convince you to buy? You were online, minding your business, and this ad pops up. Maybe it was for a t-shirt. A candle. A mattress. A card game. Something you technically did not need. But there was something about the marketing that caught your eye. You followed the ad to a website. Maybe there was a video there. It could have made you laugh. It could have made you tear up a bit. Maybe you just breathed a sigh of relief. You felt something. Happiness. Excitement. Possibility. So you bought it. And you felt great about it.

The company got you. They finessed you in some way. They didn't pressure you. They set something sexy in front of you and walked away. No pitch. No, "You're gonna die if you don't buy this!" That in itself is different. You felt eased into the sale. That approach is so opposite of what you're used to in traditional sales that you're instantly intrigued. It was different.

Your consumers are tired of seeing the same thing. They've seen a lot, and they've heard a lot. They're being beat over the head with marketing messages all day. What can you do to push the envelope a bit?

It's disruptive. UnCloned Marketing campaigns are cutting edge. An UnCloned Marketing campaign stops people in their tracks. You don't have to send a marching band to someone's house to pitch them (although I would LOVE it if you did!) but you can switch up your approach.

Consumers are savvy enough to know that a "free" webinar ain't really free, and that it will lead to an offer. They can predict that right after an opt-in page, they can expect a thank-you page. It's been done a million times before. So they move through your marketing with their guard up. What can you do that's unpredictable? Can you disrupt the pattern by skipping the opt-in and having potential customers DM you directly? It may seem small, but all you need is a little creative edge to get people excited enough to want to know more.

It builds anticipation. When you UnClone your marketing campaign, it feels like a steamy romance novel. Is he going to kiss her tonight? Will he be at the airport to stop her before she boards that plane and leaves him forever? Who is that mystery woman who found her way back into his life? Who's gonna get stabbed? Okay, that is a little more murder mystery, but you get my point. Those are the kinds of books that you don't want to put down. You're at stoplights trying to read to see what happens next. You look up and it's two o'clock in the morning, and you're still in it.

Your marketing should feel the exact same way. At every touchpoint of your campaign, you want to build so much anticipation and excitement that your customer can't wait to see what happens next.

It calls your people. Great marketing calls the people who are meant to hear it.

Let's say a fitness instructor decides to teach classes naked. That may gross some people out. Some people will clutch their pearls and call the FCC or the President of the United States to try to shut her business down. But there will be some people who absolutely love it. They may be nudists. Or people who work on Wall Street in stuffy suits and offices all day, and just want to be free and uninhibited in some area of their lives. There is something for everybody. If you show up as you, the people who want to be a part of it will come, regardless of how crazy it looks to anyone else.

There are a million gospel choirs and Christian churches in

the world, but there is something about the way the choir at Kanye West's Sunday Service sings and gives praise that draws people in droves. There are hundreds of sportswear brands, but Beyoncé's Ivy Park collaboration with Adidas was so sick that it shut down the Internet with sales. Kylie Jenner took cosmetics and her unique point of view on beauty and made a billion dollars. These are all people who took a concept—religion, sportswear, cosmetics—and made it their own. They took a risk. And the people responded.

It does not leave your audience to figure anything out.
Just because someone comes to your website and is interested in what you sell, you cannot assume they know why they need it. Even for the most obvious product, like clothes, consumers want to be educated. And they want to be able to envision themselves in whatever they are buying. UnCloned campaigns bring people into a full experience.

There is a reason why couture fashion brands still do runway shows to debut their next collections. They spend millions of dollars to bring these mega productions to life, and to bring audiences into their over-the-top worlds. They fly in fashion enthusiasts, celebrities, media, and influencers, knowing that they'll promote what they see. Some would say, why not just throw the clothes on a website? Because it's not sexy enough. It's not an experience. In a live activation or experience, people get to allow their imaginations to run wild. They become someone else as they see themselves transform through your results. They can see it all play out, from beginning to end.

If you consider these principles when you are thinking

through your campaign, you will not lose.

BUT WHAT ABOUT YOU? YOU GOTTA UNCLONE TOO

With your campaign, you will be pushing people to open up their minds to see something they've never seen before. But to do that, you have to open up too. As the lovely ladies of En Vogue crooned back in the day, "Free your miiiiiind, and the rest with follow." Here's the remix—free your mind, and your marketing will follow.

These are some ways to free your mind and make some mindset and business shifts that will set you up for success:

Be willing to challenge the norms. In case you haven't guessed it by now, I'll be beating this drum as loud as I can for the rest of this book. You have to be willing to do it differently.

I rarely tell people to stop reading one of my books, but if you are rigid and determined to stick to marketing the way you always have or how you've always seen it done, you can put this book down and pass it on to an open-minded business friend. But I promise, if you are willing to challenge your beliefs, everything that you've learned, heard, and internalized about marketing, business, and even yourself, you will be different at the end of this. In all of the best ways possible.

Be willing to go to the edge. Be willing to open your mind, put your business blinders on, and do you. Be willing to push your creativity to the max. When you come up with an idea, don't settle for basic. Challenge yourself to go bigger. Push it just a little more. See what else you can create. And keep doing that until you get to greatness.

Be willing to spend money and time. While I talk about a number of tools, resources, and approaches for your marketing campaigns in this book, from low-to-high tech, I want you to wrap your mind around the fact that you will need some budget to execute and implement. I can't tell you exactly what that budget needs to be, but I can tell you it's more than $0.00. So be prepared to put up some paper to do your campaign right.

On that same note, you have to be willing to spend some time with this too. Not just to read this book, but to do the work in these pages. To build a marketing campaign in the right way, you have to be committed to it. Roll up your sleeves, get that laptop, and get to work.

Be willing to flop. Being UnCloned means you are good with the outcome, whether it flies or flops. You cannot challenge norms and be afraid to fail. It's impossible. You also can't be so tied to the possibility of future failures that you lose sight of your present. Be here. Focus on what is in front of you. What you are about to create and do could work like gangbusters. It could set the world on fire. You won't know until you try.

GETTING YOUR CREATIVITY FLOWING AND GOING

I may be a little biased, but, to me, marketing is the most exciting part of business.

It's where you get to be creative and free. Marketing is how you can express yourself and your individuality. You can challenge the way people think, see, and experience things. Your marketing is where you get to play.

With marketing, you can let your imagination go. Have fun with it. Sit at your laptop and create by yourself, or brainstorm with your team. Go outside into the sunshine and fresh air for inspiration. Do whatever you need to do to get yourself pumped. Get outside of the box creatively. Make marketing your playground.

Here are some cool ways to spark your creativity and get inspired as you are building your campaign:

- Watch fashion runway shows.

- Watch blockbuster movie trailers.

- Research big media companies, like Disney and Netflix, and see what they're doing now and next.

- Study sportswear brands that are always launching in fresh ways.

- Look at industry icons who are always pushing the envelope with their marketing campaigns.

Creativity is like a muscle—it has to be constantly conditioned. You have just as much creativity in you as the next person. Let it out.

IT'S NOT YOUR BUDGET, IT'S YOUR BRAIN

Marketing is not just for big companies with big budgets.

As a small business, I don't want you to limit yourself or count yourself out when it comes to marketing. There is so much you can do. All you have to do is be willing to take your brain where it's never been before. You have to get creative.

What makes an UnCloned launch different, of course, is the creativity that you infuse it with. An UnCloned launch differs from the way everyone else does it because of the excitement it creates for you and your audience. Your launch should feel energetic, like a blockbuster movie. If done right, there should be hype and hysteria surrounding it. It should be an experience the world cannot wait to watch unfold.

Think about a company that is legendary for their launches, like Apple. Whenever a new version of the iPhone is released, it's one of the biggest events in the technology industry. Bloggers fly in. Media covers the event to make it front-page news. It's a big deal. It's UnCloned.

I know what you're thinking—you don't have an Apple budget. Let's be real, money helps. But it's not everything. You can be creative and intentional about your launch, without spending a rack of money. If you don't have big money now, someday you will. In the meantime, let's make the biggest splash possible with what you have. We'll get into how to get the most bang for your marketing bucks more in the chapters to come, but what I want you to understand now is that budget is important, but you don't have to sit by and do nothing with your marketing if you don't have a lot of it.

- Maybe you can't afford to produce an all-out video series, but you can fire up that phone and teach your butt off on an Instagram Live.

- Maybe you can't afford to give away free lobsters dinners to everyone in the neighborhood, but you can host a few well-known food bloggers and influencers in your restaurant so they can get conversations popping about how great their experience was.

- Maybe you can't afford to hire a graphic designer to re-brand your entire business, but you can find a freelancer to create a few amazing graphics for the offer you are about to launch so you wow people with what they will see first.

See my point?

You don't always need millions of dollars or a big team behind you to make a marketing campaign successful. The majority of my launches, many of which have made six figures or more, were executed with me and one or two people supporting me. I've never had a huge launch team. But what I did have was creativity and consistency.

Whenever I am planning a launch, I like to ask myself, *What would the gurus do? What would I do if I had the cash? What would Steve Jobs or Richard Branson do? If money, people, or time was no object, what would I create?*

I want you to start thinking that way too. Put yourself in the shoes of CEOs with unlimited resources, people, and marketing budgets. Unleash your creativity first, and then figure out how to pay for it. I can assure you there is a way to scale your idea to match your budget.

Creativity is free—and the results are priceless.

LET THE WORK BEGIN, BABY: THE UNCLONED MARKETING CAMPAIGN SUCCESS PATH

By now, you should be feeling pumped, inspired, and *ready ready* to build the most UnCloned, crazy profitable marketing campaign that the world has ever seen.

Now that we've done the mindset work, it's time to put in that marketing work.

In this book, I am teaching you my UnCloned Marketing Campaign Success Path, which is my proven method for launching anything.

The Success Path is a set of six important steps that every business should follow to create a successful campaign. These are the building blocks to create a solid foundation for your entire campaign.

Do them all, and you are destined for success. Skip one, and your whole campaign will go from top-notch to trash. Here's a sneak peek of exactly what we are about to get into:

Step One—Authority and Credibility. This step is about establishing yourself in the market. I'll give you the toolkit for getting people to know, love, and respect you in your industry.

Step Two—Offers. Once people are clear on who you are and why you are the obvious choice for them, we'll walk through how to sell and craft an UnCloned product, service, event, or experience that people want.

Step Three—Lead Generation Strategy. Now you're ready to bring people to your thing. We'll discuss specific strategies for increasing eyeballs and visibility for your offer and your entire campaign.

Step Four—Marketing Plan. This step is all things marketing. You'll walk away with a well-thought-out plan so you are not winging it through your launch.

Step Five—Launching and Sales. Here, we'll cover what you need to do to prepare yourself for your launch, and the art of selling once you get in front of people.

Step Six—Mastering Your Clients and Customers. Getting customers to buy is just the beginning of your sale. You are still selling through your customer service and experience. We'll get into how to keep your customers happy and what you can do to position them for the next sale in the process.

Are you ready? I know you are. Flip this page and jump right in.

"Be Willing to Challenge the Norms."

- Audria Richmond

CHAPTER FOUR
AUTHORITY AND CREDIBILITY

I have a question for you:

When was the last time you gave someone anything of value without verifying who they were first?

Think about it.

Whether we are talking about your money, your Mama's-Momma's-Momma's pound cake recipe, or your hand in marriage, whenever we give up something we consider to be important, we want to be sure we can trust the person we are sharing our valuables with. We want them to protect it, respect it, and cherish it, just like we would. We don't want them to run off with that thing and misuse it. And more than that, we want them to hold up their end of the bargain.

If we loan money, we expect it to be repaid. If we share how to bake that cake, we expect the friend we gave a sacred family recipe to take the secret to her grave. If we exchange vows with a partner, we expect they will honor the union. These are all situations that come up in life, but the same rules apply in business.

No one is going to pay you for anything if they don't trust you or believe you can—and will—do what you said you would do.

When consumers are considering the company they should choose, they want to feel safe. They want to trust that the person on the other end of the transaction is capable, consistent, and credible. From the moment they encounter your business, be it through your website, a video ad, a conversation at the counter of your burger spot, or holding your hand-made soaps at farmer's market, people want to feel assured they are in great hands with you. They may not be conveying their concerns to you verbally, but trust me, their minds are racing a mile a minute with questions:

Do you know what you're talking about?

Will you disappear with my money once I've entered my credit card?

Will you ship my product?

Is your product quality great?

Your food looks mighty tasty on Instagram. But how will it look and taste when I get to your restaurant?

How are you qualified to do what you do?

Are you the expert you appear to be?

These are the questions that your audience is really asking. Your marketing has to give them the answers.

If you read my book, *Are You Ready for the Yes: How to Prep Your Brand for Lucrative Opportunities*, you'll know that I devoted each and every one of those pages to laying out everything you need to build a personal brand the right way. In the book, I break down the must-haves of a powerful, profitable, personal brand, like a professionally designed website and branded images. It's no secret that, as a professional graphic designer and photographer, I believe that top-notch visual branding is an essential part of every small business's success formula. But as a marketing and launch strategist who is here to teach you how to get to the money, I have to tell you that, while important, your beautiful graphics and pictures are just the beginning. And if you stop there, your bucks will too.

This is why establishing your authority and credibility in the marketplace is the first step to building a profitable marketing campaign.

Selling without establishing authority and credibility first is a sure-fire way to kill your shot at a sale. You cannot make money if people are wondering if you're legit. If your audience is even the slightest bit skeptical about you, you can cancel Christmas. Make it easy for people to trust you. Offer them proof up front so they don't have to work for it.

We all know from personal experience how critical credibility is. Why? Because we've all been burned by somebody who we found out was not who they presented themselves to be, particularly online. They looked, smelled, and sounded good, but once you gave them your money, you found out they were a complete fraud. Ask anybody who has been on the dating scene recently who's been straight catfished or hired an unskilled contractor to finish their kitchen—and they're still washing dishes in their tub two years later.

People want to know for sure that you are who you say you are, especially in business. We live in a world where people can present themselves in any way they want to. So consumers are demanding more than smoke and mirrors. They are researching, asking around for references—and checking them—and looking for proof of the results you've created not just for yourself, or just anybody else, but people who have the exact same problem they have. They are peeking behind the curtains of pretty websites and graphics to find out what type of knowledge and experience is there. They are watching your YouTube videos, combing through your social media, and checking for proof of your expertise. They are reading online reviews of your product on Yelp and Google. The average consumer is getting much smarter about who they spend their money with, spotting lies, and avoiding fakers and frauds.

So that means you have to go harder to prove you are not one of them.

ALL EYES ON YOU

In this world-wide-web-driven globe that we live on, people are just a few keystrokes away from learning everything they need to know about you. The world sees you, and their inquiring minds want to know what you do and how you do it.

So if you are selling a service, your personal brand is super important.

Contrary to popular belief, your personal brand's job is not to talk about how much you love expensive lattes, luxury vacations, cars, and homes. This is not about personality—it's about proof. You want to build a personal brand that consistently demonstrates you are legit and convince people you know your 'ish.

For my service-based peeps, think about your personal brand as one big billboard that sells yourself as an expert and authority in the market. When your potential people are checking you out, here are some hallmarks of a tried-and-true expert that they're looking for:

- **A platform that showcases your expertise**. Experts have endless amounts of proof that they know their stuff. They have videos, blogs, books—tangible content to prove they can create a result.

- **You can talk the talk.** One of the first signs that you're in front of a pro is how fluent they are in what they do. Give them five minutes or five hours, and a true expert can break down a topic they know well so convincingly and easily that you cannot wait to pay them for more. Oprah can talk about media all day. Denzel can do the same with acting. When someone has mastered their craft, they don't blink or stutter when given an opportunity to tell someone else about it. You should be able to carry an in-depth conversation about what you do.

- **You've been doing this for a minute.** Real experts have likely been working their craft for a minute. It's not to say that someone cannot ramp up their knowledge quickly, but it takes some time and hard work to build a reputation, complete several successful projects, and build a body of work.

- **You have receipts.** We'll get into this a little more in this chapter, but never forget the necessity of proving you can get a result for people. Successful service-based businesses can show who they've performed a service for in the past. Receipts always speak louder than your words and are the easiest way to prove you know how to do what you say you can do.

If you are selling a product, in addition to showing up and showcasing your expertise, your potential customers are particularly honed in on how your product looks, feels, and performs. Product-based companies have to ensure the story that is being told about their goods is solid as a rock. Your online rep is everything. Here are two big clues your potential customers are looking for to determine if your product is as great as you claim it is:

Online Reviews. Before someone tries your product blindly—meaning no one they know and trust has vouched for it yet—you can best believe they are making a beeline to see what others say about it. Google and Yelp reviews are very telling, and we all know that, in this day and age, people don't hold anything back when given an opportunity to vent about or praise a company. Before people buy what you're selling, they want to know some things. What are other people saying about their experience with your product? How did the burger in your restaurant taste? Were the servers friendly and helpful? How clean were the tables? If you are in retail, did the t-shirt turn into a pile of thread in the dryer? Like it or not, reviews can make or break a business.

Social Media. A customer can tell a lot about your business from what they see on social. It's been said that a picture is worth a thousand words, and, in business, a picture can be worth a thousand dollars—or more—too. If you have a brick-and-mortar business, like a restaurant or a spa, enticing images of your food, products, and space are what will get people in the door. If you have an online boutique, great pictures of your clothes sell. Creative captions and product descriptions are important, but those images should speak too.

STANDING OUT IN A CROWDED MARKETPLACE

Aside from making a positive, and ultimately profitable, impression on your audience, your authority and credibility is also important to distinguish yourself from your competition. It may feel like there are thousands of people who do what you do, and you're absolutely right. Your potential customers have options—lots of them. And at this point in the game, there will be plenty of them who've invested in their visual branding and teeth whitening, so their websites and smiles are just as bright as yours. So how will a consumer know who is the real expert and who is faking the funk? It comes back to authority and credibility. When your game is tight, you will be the cream that rises to the top.

With plenty of people to choose from, your customer's heads may be spinning as they are trying to decide which company is best for them. But you can position yourself as the obvious choice with these **10 Ways to Distinguish Yourself in the Market:**

1. **Products and Services.** What you sell is an easy way to stand out in the market. Are you coming with something different from other businesses that do what you do?

2. **Packaging and Presentation.** How does your customer receive your product or service? Do you toss your t-shirts in a basic, black, plastic bag, or do you put them in an

inflated balloon that has to be popped first? Are your vegan sandwiches served on a bed of edible grass instead of wrapped in parchment paper? Are your emails well-branded? These are little touches that make a big difference.

3. **Pricing.** How does your price stack up against everyone else's? And keep in mind this does not necessarily mean the cheapest. Yes, some people are looking for a bargain and the budget-friendly option, but others are less cost-conscious and only care about having the best. Premium pricing usually signals quality. If your prices are higher than everyone else's, people may choose you for that reason.

4. **Creativity.** Never underestimate the power of some excitement. When people encounter something they've never seen before, they want more. People will pay a premium for something that stands out from all of their other options.

5. **Doing business with you.** Consumers are judging your systems and processes. Complicated websites and sales funnels are a turn off. You can have the better offer, but if your competitors make it easy to do business with them, people will go over there for simplicity and less stress.

6. **Marketing.** Studies show that the person who shows up the most wins. Your competitors may be beating you to the money because they are simply more visible. Are you marketing frequently, or are you only showing up once a year? Do you have a podcast, are you publishing ex-

pert-level content, a show, or a magazine? How often people see you matters. Even if they are not ready to buy, consistent marketing keeps you top of mind for when they are.

7. **Convenience.** How convenient is your offering? In today's world, people want what they need right at their fingertips. Can people buy from you through an app? Is your store right in the neighborhood so they can skip a trip to the mall that is twenty minutes away? The closer you are to the people who need you, the more money you'll make.

8. **Need.** This is so important that it really should be number one on this list. If you do not convince your potential customers and clients they need what you sell, you will find it hard to seal the deal. Right before they swipe their credit card, consumers are always asking themselves, "Do I actually need this?" This is a question you have to answer to convince your potential clients and customers to choose you. How is your thing solving a pressing problem in their lives? Your competition may be lacking here. Slide in there with a strong argument that makes people want and need what you sell now and you've got the sale.

9. **Positioning** in the marketplace in comparison to your competition. You can be the absolute best at what you do, but that doesn't mean you're the only one doing it. This is why positioning is so important. How are you showing up?

10. **Authority and Credibility.** Taking over the market as an

expert, becoming your audience's go-to, and flooding the airwaves with proof of your skills, value, quality, and results is a sure-fire way to stand out in the sea of sameness. That proof that you are the real deal will always put you paces ahead of your fake—I am just saying—competition.

YOUR PROFITS ARE IN YOUR PROOF

Nothing says "Pay me!" better than proof that your products and services actually work. We are in the age of show and tell, so your potential clients and customers are looking for actual results. Whether you are selling after school fun for kids, a fitter body, or better finances, people want to be assured they are getting what they pay for.

Everything else you do to stand out and market your business won't matter if you can't show that your thing can do its thing. You gotta give proof. The success of your entire marketing campaign, especially your sales, depends on it.

Here's how you package the proof that shows people that, above all else, you get results:

- **Personal Results.** Is your own life or business a reflection of what you do? Putting your methods or products to work for yourself and sharing your own results is a must. When you sell a course that guarantees increased social media engagement, your pages and feeds should be popping with likes and comments. When you are a skincare expert with a product line, your skin's glow should speak for itself. You should always be a walking advertisement for your business.

- **Before and Afters.** How many times have you done a double take when you saw a side-by-side image of someone who has lost a drastic amount of weight? When you can show visually how you were able to take someone from Point A to Point B—or maybe even Point Z—you replace questions about your credibility with cash. People love a good struggle-to-success story, especially when they can see themselves in it and visualize a similar result for themselves.

- **Case Studies.** Case studies are a tool that big companies use all the time, and one that small business can leverage too. Similar to a before and after, case studies give a detailed, usually written, account of how a client came through your door, the process that you took them through, and how they improved as a result.

- **Reviews and Testimonials.** You can toot your horn all day—and you should—but positive reviews and testimonials are priceless in marketing. Who else is saying that you're dope? Has word gotten around that you are the go-to man or woman for the job, and everywhere you go, there are people singing your praises? This is the type of credibility that every business wants and needs. You want people who gush about the great experience they've had with your company and are willing to recommend you to others.

- **Behind-the-Scenes Video Content.** Letting people into your lab and showing how you build and create is powerful proof of your authority and credibility. There are a lot of business owners who want to keep their knowledge under wraps. Transparency can show your potential clients and customers that you are bold enough to give value and that you know your stuff inside out.

- **Interviews and Original Content.** Raise your hand to be interviewed on credible platforms. Produce that podcast. Document your next big product launch in a video series. Create conversations that demonstrate your expertise and results.

- **Authoring a Book.** I could talk about the value of publishing your own books for the rest of my life. Becoming an author makes you an instant industry authority and establishes your credibility through your knowledge. So get to writing!

If you can work any—or all—of these into your marketing campaign...baby! You are cooking with some real gas.

GETTING IT WHEN YOU AIN'T GOT IT—YET

Okay, so if you just read the list above and there is nothing you can check off just yet, don't stress. Your business isn't doomed to fail just because you don't have enough experience under your belt yet to pull this level of proof together to showcase your results. You may still be toying with an idea for a business or feeling brand new to what you do. And while it may seem that everything you've read is for established entrepreneurs, I want you to know this book is for you too.

You have something of value to offer the world. Your skill set or product may be new, but your desire to serve and succeed is not. You are already well on your way. And besides, we all have to start somewhere. So you can start *here* with building authority and credibility if you don't have it. All you have to do is follow these four tips to get ramped up to pro level:

1. **Research and Data.** If you don't know what you need to know, it's time to go learn it. With so much access to information and expertise, you can become an authority on anything. If you want to learn how to produce the best webinars so you can teach others, go to YouTube and devour videos. If you want to become a photographer to help people take better dating profile pictures, go read blogs and articles on the topic. The more you know, the more credible you are. Study, study, and study some more.

   Next, you need data that proves all this research and methods actually work, which leads me to my next point...

2. **Hands-on/Real-World Experience.** If you say you know how to build websites, you want to be able to point your potential client to a portfolio where they can see your work in action. If you have an idea for a hair oil that grows hair, get in the kitchen. Get out there and gets your hands dirty. Design. Mix. Create. Teach. Practice on some people. Do your thing as much as possible until you become a guru.

3. **Education + Hands-on/Real-World Experience.** If you went to school to study a particular thing, then you have knowledge to build on. Put that degree or certification

to work and start practicing what you've learned in the classroom.

4. **Leverage Someone Else's Authority and Credibility.** This is ideal for experts who don't have a big enough platform or audience of their own yet. Find fellow experts, leaders, and strategic partners who complement what you do. Collaborate with them and get in front of their people.

MASTERING YOUR MARKETING MESSAGE

When it's time to sell your product or service, you need to be able to talk to people about it.

As you develop your marketing campaign, you will be continuously speaking to audiences about your offering. And when you are in front of someone who you want to take action, what you don't want is a conversation full of theoretical mumbo-jumbo—also known as talking out of your butt. For your marketing message to be effective, you want to speak straight facts. Your knowledge, experience, the in-depth research you've gathered on who your customer is and what they need, along with your proven ability to deliver results, are all valuable pieces of data that will help you to craft a marketing message that makes people want to move. The more people you work with, the more information you have in your arsenal to use.

But first, you need to learn how to speak their language. Nothing excites a customer more when they hear someone who gets them. When you can prove that you get their problem and, more importantly, have their solution in hand, you'll have their attention.

As an expert, it is tempting to speak to audiences from your point of view. But when you put your marketing hat on, you need to speak from theirs. And speaking your customer's language is much easier when you hear it straight from their mouths. So your job is to get people talking and listen when they do.

Let me help you with some ways to do that:

- **Ask questions that encourage open-ended responses.** When you are talking to clients, asking questions such as, "What are you struggling with most?" or "What made you want to hire a strategist?" opens the door for people to tell you what they need, versus you guessing.

- **Pay attention to concerns and FAQs**. If your customers are continuously running into the same roadblocks and struggles, or asking the same questions on repeat, those are signals about the types of problems they need you to help them solve and the results they are looking for.

- **Take notes on calls.** As you are leading customers through your process, be sure to have your pen and paper ready. Every meeting and call are opportunities for you to learn more about your customer's needs.

- **Read comments and messages.** Social media is a goldmine for customer insights. Play detective a little bit. Poke around and check out comments on posts and in groups—both yours and your competitors'—and see what people are talking and ranting about.

With all the intel you've gathered, you're ready to put this thing into words.

Now, I know you are a pro, but now is not the time for flowery, creative, or even technical talk. You want a marketing message that is jargon-free and easy to understand. A marketing message is worthless if it's so over-the-top that it leaves people scratching their heads and unable to figure out what you do. People want to know what you offer as quickly as possible so they can make a quick decision about whether or not they need it. Keep in mind that the longer your sales pitch is, the longer it will take you to get to the money.

You may have various versions of your marketing message to use for different purposes. For example, my marketing message is:

I'm the woman everyone comes to when they want to stand out from the crowd and stop using cookie cutter marketing strategies and tactics in the marketplace. I strategically coach, consult, and advise forward-thinking executives, brands, and creatives on how to UnClone themselves creatively so that they can increase their brand awareness and generate revenue.

When I am short on time and need to keep my text to a minimum, I may use an alternate version that says something like:

If you want an #UnCloned Edge with the launch of your

next product, service, or event, I can help you develop creative, strategic, and profitable #UnCloned Marketing Campaigns.

And then when I have to get right, right to it, I'll say:

I help my clients launch creative, strategic, and profitable #UnCloned Marketing Campaigns.

Here are some plug-and-play templates that you can use:

If you sell services:

I help (insert the people you work with) to (insert the result of using your service).

Example: I help married couples create more spark in the bedroom.

If you sell products:

I sell (insert the type of product) that (insert the result of using your product).

Example: I sell all-natural soaps that cleanse, exfoliate, and moisturize skin in one step.

Start playing with your marketing message and drilling it down until it's compelling, clear, and concise. Become a pro at talking to people about what you do.

You'll be doing it *a lot*.

ALLOW ME TO INTRODUCE MYSELF

If you've read to this point, and you've been in business for some time, you may be thinking these are all boxes that you've already checked. Being well-known and regarded in some spaces is great, but to grow your business, you should be constantly launching new offers and searching for new markets to penetrate. This means marketing yourself to new audiences again and again.

The need for authority and credibility is essential whether you are brand new to business or pivoting into a new market.

If the people who you want to pay you don't know who you are, it does not matter if you've established yourself in other markets with other customers. You still have to show and prove to the new audience that you want to reach today. You may be a rock star in other markets, but it doesn't matter to the people who've never experienced your work. Sure, they may Google you and learn a little about you. But the fact that you mastered one aspect of the market does not mean your name and expertise carries weight in another. Yes, you may be the most qualified company in the market. But you can't expect to show up in a strange place, be it online or in a completely new sector, and want people to pay you.

In the last ten years, I've had to reestablish my authority and credibility with each pivot I made in my business. My first businesses were established in Memphis. I had a great following there, but when I decided to expand my business into personal branding and come online, I had to introduce myself to a completely new audience and build credibility. The same was the case when I started moving into the corporate space. I'd had incredible success working with hundreds of entrepreneurs and small business owners, but big corporate was brand new for me. Bigger companies do business differently. So establishing authority and credibility in that industry meant I had to show and prove my value in working with larger organizations.

I'll use another example—my dad. He is an incredible mechanic who has been fixing cars practically all his life. He can diagnose a problem with a car with his eyes closed. But outside of his family and friends, no one knows who he is. If he decided to go legit and introduce himself on a massive platform and start a business, he would need to build a brand from the ground up. He would have to establish his credibility as a mechanic beyond his neighborhood. New markets and new audiences mean new intros.

Don't assume that people know you, regardless of how big of a following you have somewhere else.

With consistency in your marketing, particularly in establishing authority and credibility, brand recognition will come. If Coca-Cola or Pepsi launch a new canned, diet drink that slims your waistline in six weeks, you likely would not think twice about buying it tomorrow. That's because both of their brands are so recognizable in the marketplace. They've established the authority and credibility that has made them mainstays in the market. When you buy a Coke or Pepsi product, you know, in general, what to expect. You know the quality and the taste. You don't expect to open a can with their logo on it and taste garbage.

This new get-sexy-and-slim-by-summer drink may be the

worst thing you've ever tasted, but the point is you were willing to pay for it and try it on the strength of their authority and credibility in the market.

[insert your small business name here], LLC., is much different from Coca-Cola. Until we can establish ourselves as a brand the way that Coke, Pepsi, and other big brands have, we have some work to do. It's not to say that your soda, service, or whatever it is that you sell is not just as good. But it's not as known. And that means we have a little more work to do. We have to prove to the people who don't know who we are what we can do.

Keep beating the drum until your respect, recognition, and money come.

That, my friends, is great marketing.

Take Action

Before you move on to the next chapter, do this:

- Make a list of all the proof that showcases you as an expert and supports what you want to be known and paid for.

- If you are new to business, and you don't have a strong portfolio of proof to showcase your expertise and results yet, go get it.

- Get your money-making marketing message down pat.

CHAPTER FIVE
FREE AND PAID OFFERS

In the simplest business terms, an offer is a physical or digital product, service, event, or experience that results in more people or more money.

As a business, your end game is not always revenue—at least not immediately. You may be creating an offer to grow your audience. Perhaps you are focused on growing your platform, so your goal is to get listeners for your new podcast, followers on social media, or readers for a newsletter. Then there are times when your primary goal is to grow your bottom line, and you are creating an offer to make money.

Whether you are selling an opportunity to be part of your community or audience or to buy something from you, you are still creating an offer that you want to get to the masses. And it needs to be fire.

Let's get into how you create offers, and of course, how to make them UnCloned.

THE FREE OFFER

A free offer—also known as a freebie, an opt-in, or a lead magnet—attracts leads or people who you ideally can convert into your paid product or service. They are not customers, clients, subscribers, or followers *yet*. By giving people an opportunity to know, like, and trust you with something free, they can test-drive what you sell or do before committing to rock with you (ta-da, trust). Free offers are powerful pieces of marketing. If done right, they can practically seal the sale.

Your free offer should:

- **Handle the first step in the process of educating your**

customer. Remember, marketing is about educating and informing your customer. Think about what you say on a consultation call or if you met a potential client for the first time. What would they need to know? Build a free offer to answer all their questions.

- **Handle the objection.** What stands in the way of you and the sale? What are your potential clients or customers struggling with? Use your free offer to get them over the hump, whatever that is.

  For example, if you are an intellectual property attorney, you may find that most entrepreneurs have no idea what is considered intellectual property. Your free offer could be a free workshop to help them identify what types of intellectual property they have. At the end of that workshop, you would offer a paid legal consultation to discuss what they discovered and how your services could help them protect their assets.

- **Handle the first step of the sale.** If your offer does all the above, your ideal customer should only have one question: "Where do I sign up?" Free offers ideally make your sales and onboarding process that much easier and eliminate the need for lots of questions and hard-core convincing to tempt people to buy or take action.

YOUR FREE SHOULD STILL FEEL EXPENSIVE

In an UnCloned marketing campaign, you want to place just as much energy and effort into your free offer as you do a paid offer. Both should feel like a high-quality experience.

Keep in mind that you are setting the stage for what your customer can expect if they were to pay you or come into your community. They're looking for a sample of what they can expect once they actually pay you for your product or service. You have to make it well worth their time, energy, and especially their money.

It's a simple example, but think about your last trip to a mall. If you were in the food court, there was probably someone standing in front of a booth, offering you a bite of food. A salesperson from a cosmetics kiosk stepped out in your path and offered you a packet of free face cream. It's not un-common for retailers to send big, thick catalogs during the holidays. These aren't cheap to produce, but the companies understand the huge possibility for a return on their invest-ment. If customers get excited enough about what they see on those pages, the company will make their money back tenfold in sales.

Free offers are not free to produce. They are going to cost you some money, but a quality free offer is one of the best investments you can possibly make in your business. The more excited consumers are about your free offer, the more likely they are to drool over your paid offer. Give them an experi-ence that is so damn good, they can't wait to throw money at your feet.

There are tons of options for free offers. Some of my favor-ites are:

- 1-on-1 Calls

- LIVEStreams

- Online and Offline Workshops

- Challenges

- Video Series

- Webinars

- Meetups

- Memberships

- Audits and Assessments

- Audiobooks

- Print Books and Workbooks

- Done for You Resources

- Newsletters

- Magazines

- Software Tools

- Coupons/Discount Codes

- Trial Offers

THE PAID OFFER

If your free offer is done right, your clients won't be able to wait to experience your paid offer. Once they get to this point in the process, the anticipation of the reveal should have them on the edge of their seats. And your job is to make sure it was worth the wait.

As with free offers, the sky is the limit when it comes to paid offers. **Anything that you see on the list of free offers in the previous section could easily become a paid offer.** Or you can consider any of the following:

- Virtual/Live Events and Conferences

- Speaking

- Audio Series/Course

- Podcast/Podcast Series

- Physical and Digital Templates

- VIP Day/Weeks/Weekends

- Masterminds

- Streaming Services

- Products (such as courses, food, beauty products, electronics)

Your paid offers should be positioned, packaged, and presented in such a way that you are the obvious choice for your customer. Keep in mind that, by the time a potential customer encounters you, they've been around—not necessarily in terms of dates, but definitely in terms of marketing. It doesn't matter if you are selling socks or cleaning services for Hollywood mansions, your potential customers have likely shopped, or at least seen, your competitors. They've seen an ad or commercial. They've gone online and looked at other companies. Somewhere, they've seen somebody who sells what you sell or does what you do.

This is why how you show up is so important.

UNCLONING YOUR OFFERS

Deciding what to offer takes time and lots of creativity. You know we do it UnCloned around here, so this is the part of your campaign where you really want to put on your thinking cap, let the ideas flow, and don't stop until you create something that will blow your potential customers and clients away—and your competition out of the water.

As you are crafting your offer, there are some questions to help you make it UnCloned:

Have I seen this before? If you can look around and see five hundred versions of exactly what you're offering, you have to go back to the creative drawing board. A great offer is something that people haven't seen before. Do it differently—or don't do it at all.

What additional value can I add to take my offer over the top? In other words, what can I add to my offer that is so crazy expensive, it completely knocks out my cheap competitors? Most business owners are looking for ways to cut costs, not increase them. So they want to offer the least and charge the most. But you are not like everybody else. It's easy to follow the crowd, but to win in business, you have to capitalize on what everyone else is not doing. Go insane. If you are hosting a conference, can you charter a yacht to bring your attendees to the venue? Can you design a glow-in-the-dark bottle for your melatonin-infused bedtime tea? These are the types of crazy ideas that may cost you some money, but they will take your offer—and your profits—completely over the top and smoke your competition.

What could I include that people would never see coming? People love a surprise. Adding something unexpected to your offer will take it over the top.

What type of intellectual property can I create that will block others from taking my idea? You want to make your offer so distinct—and legally bulletproof—that your sneaky, there-is-no-way-they-are-doper-than-you competitors can't snatch it from you. This goes for your logo, brand colors, and assets. Weave all of these elements into your offer. And then hire an intellectual property attorney to help you protect it.

What industries can I remix with my brand to give me a creative edge? Looking outside of your industry can help you to craft a distinct offer. If you are in the beauty industry, what tactics can you borrow from the car industry when it comes to how they bring new, flashy cars to the market? If you are in the legal industry, what's the latest in fashion that you can leverage? Look around. You are bound to find some creative ideas for offers.

What are others unwilling to do? This means pushing the envelope in your industry. What looks like a loss in profits to some, could be the offer that sets you up for millions. For example, if you are a hairstylist, could you do unlimited styles for a flat rate? This is something that your regular customers will love for the ease and convenience and completely disrupt your industry.

What could I offer for free? Giving away something for free, especially if it's perceived to be of high value, will wow your customers and leave your competitors dumbfounded. One of my favorite offers is to give away my book for free. While other authors are hawking customers for $19.99, I am offering my book at no cost in exchange for their information to build my lists and community, and to eventually upsell those people into paid products and services. Don't be so afraid to give something away. If you do it right, it will be well worth it. (More on this later in this chapter.)

How can I include some really unique tech? Even if you don't consider yourself a techie, your customers probably are. Incorporating technology into your offer adds a thrill factor. If you have an online boutique, how dope would it be to create a virtual reality shop for customers to come in and try your new collection in a luxury store without leaving their homes? Do some research online and in technology-focused magazines and publications to see what new gadgets, software, and strategies are out there that you can play with and incorporate into your offer.

How can I package my offer in an unconventional way? Later in this chapter, I get into some amazing examples of brands who do this right. But you want to, once again, think about the unexpected.

How can you get your client a win so they can bring you more business? Exploring collaborations and strategic partnerships is a great way to do this. Offering to be of service to someone whose product or service complements yours is great business, increases your flow of referrals, and can add value to offer if the two of you decide to market together. So, if you sell wedding dresses, could you partner with a personal trainer to help your brides slim down in time to shop for gowns? If you are in real estate, can you collaborate with a credit repair company to get clients ready to purchase a home? Regardless of what you do, there are hundreds of ways to team up with other businesses to bring more business in the door and to stand out.

How can I take an unconventional approach to fixing an issue for my client or an issue in society as a whole? Your offer should solve a problem, but that doesn't mean it has to be boring. Just when you think you've reached the epitome of dope, trust me, *you can go doper*. As a therapist, can you start making house calls or maybe see clients in a spa so they can really relax? Think of uncommon, UnCloned ways that you can deliver the services that people consistently use and need in a way that they've never seen before.

In case you haven't guessed it, UnCloning your offer comes down to one important thing—disrupting your industry.

The types of free and paid offers that I shared with you earlier in this chapter may not be new to you, but the way you put a spin on them to make them your own should be. Your packaging, positioning, and approach will turn any offer or tactic that we've seen in some way before, and make it distinct and unrecognizable. This is how companies that change the game are born.

People who are brand new to the game surpass the former front runners in their industries for one reason, and one reason alone, they created disruption. They've taken a unique approach that we have not seen before, and now, they are in a league and lane of their own.

Let's look at some of the most UnCloned companies on the planet, and what makes them distinct in the market:

Johnny Cupcakes. Johnny Cupcakes is an apparel brand that you would know from the moment you laid eyes on it. The company remixed clothing with the baking industry. Their visual branding, packaging, and store design all resemble a cupcake brand. This is genius packaging, and a completely fresh approach.

Cirque du Soleil. Cirque du Soleil is a global brand that took the circus and family entertainment world by storm. They set out to find a way to take the circus and present in a more sophisticated, magical way. With animal-like characters with stunning costumes, all-out storytelling, and thrilling aerial performances, Cirque du Soleil is undeniably UnCloned.

Shen Yun Performing Arts. A few sections back I mentioned using intellectual property as a way to UnClone your offer. Well, this company did exactly that. With a patented technology that blends dancers and performers seamlessly into the stage sets, not only is Shen Yun thrilling audiences, they are securing their position in entertainment and theater with distinct tech that no one can replicate.

The Sugar Baby Summit: Finding love is a challenge that many people face, especially those in high-profile positions. That's where the Sugar Baby Summit comes in. Presented by Seeking Arrangement, a membership-based matchmaking company, the summit is a live event where women and men who want to become Sugar Babies (paid companions for members) come to learn how to become ideal matches.

These are just a few companies that offer real-life examples of what an offer can be when disruption, distinction, and creativity are the priority. I know these are big-name brands, but even if you don't have their big budgets, you have a big imagination. Use it, unleash it, and watch what happens. Let your mind run wild, as if budget weren't a factor, and you could do any and everything you wanted to do. Start at the top, and scale back only if you have to. Find ways to improvise.

Reinvent. Reimagine. But please, *please*, don't put the brakes on your creativity. Because there is some new, fresh company whose offers I'd love to profile in my next book about the most UnCloned companies on the planet.

And I am holding a spot on that list just for you.

Now get to UnCloning.

YOUR OFFER IS MORE VALUABLE THAN YOU REALIZE

When it comes to crafting and presenting an offer, one of the biggest mistakes I see business owners make is not understanding its value. Your product or service is not just some random thing you sell. It saves people time, money, or stress.

It makes them look or feel good. It provides something, a result, that they are unable to get anywhere else. That is what they are actually paying for, not the tangible product or service.

If you are a chef, you may be providing the only healthy, satisfying meal that your customers eat all day.

If you create software or some type of technology, you are helping individuals or companies to get something done so much faster than they would have without your innovation.

If you sell cosmetics, you are helping someone to feel more sexy and confident about themselves and their appearance.

If you sell t-shirts, you are helping people to express a belief or support a cause they believe in, or look so good that they get stopped on the street and constantly complimented.

What you sell means something. It has value. It's something that somebody, somewhere, cannot live without. You are not just selling any ol' thing.

The value of your offer drives the positioning as well as the price.

THE DOLLARS ARE IN THE DETAILS

Be sure that you're conveying the full value of your offer, down to the details. That's where the dollars are. You want people to be able to see and understand the full value of what you offer. You know it's dope and you are packing in a lot of value for the investment, but your potential customers need to know that too.

How often have you seen a printed ad that displays two prices? When this happens, there is one price, the "actual" cost, and then right beside it you'll see "your" price, which is the amount the company is asking you to pay—if you sign up today for this limited-time offer. You know how it goes. It gets your attention, doesn't it? That little Jedi-mind marketing trick ensures that as a consumer, you are well aware of what the item *should* cost. When you see that, you know you are getting a deal. And so you are more inclined to buy as a result.

You don't necessarily have to play the price game, but when you are marketing your offers, you want to convey the full value, down to the details, of what the offer includes. Help people to see how much they're getting for their money.

When I was offering my UnCloned Marketing Membership, which used to be one of my flagship paid offers, members not only had access to the course content, which was incredibly valuable on its own, but there was so much more. Their membership also included additional benefits such as dedicated support, group coaching calls, and an opportunity to share their knowledge on a podcast. When I ran campaigns to market the membership to increase enrollment, I always shared all the benefits. This made my marketing easier and far more effective than a social media post with just my pretty picture on it and the investment.

While there are other marketing memberships out there that were far less than the $247 that I charged, the value I provided justified the investment. And my customers happily paid it.

As you put the final touches on your offer, get into those details. Find creative ways to give your customers more, and then put a premium price on it. In the words of Luther Vandross, it's never too much.

The more value you give, the more of an experience your offer becomes.

KILL THEM WITH THE EXPERIENCE

In this super competitive marketplace, people don't want to be satisfied—they want to be wowed. They want to be stimulated. They want to be catered to. They want to be heard and understood. They want to be exposed to something that feels fresh and new. They want their needs met and their expectations exceeded.

They want an experience.

From the visual presentation and packaging to the conversations they have with you, your people want more. That means more than what they've had in the past. More than what the next company is offering. More than the basics they paid for. So when it comes to what you sell, I want you to think bigger. How can you upgrade what you sell and how you sell it? How can you package and present an offer that is so out-of-this-world, your customer's are running to purchase it first?

It doesn't matter if you are selling a $.99 lollipop or a $350,000 Bentley, consumers want a top-notch experience. And it's the company that provides the best experience that wins, hands down, each and every time. While your competition is being basic, you have an opportunity to blow them out of the water with an amazing experience.

Experience is everything.

There is coffee from the gas station on the corner, and then there is Starbucks. There is the pop-up carnival with the raggedy rides in the shopping mall parking lot, and then there is Disneyworld. There is RedBox and then there is Netflix.

The bottom line is simple: You gotta give them more.

Recently, my husband and I celebrated my birthday at the Four Seasons hotel in Miami, Florida. From the moment we made our reservations, the experience began. It was like being in my own version of *The Wizard of Oz*. When that tornado blew Dorothy into The Land of Oz, when she woke up, she could look around at all that glitter and gold and see she wasn't in Kansas anymore. Like Dorothy, I knew, as soon as we pulled up to the front of that hotel, this would not be like any other experience I had before.

There were text messages on the day prior to our arrival, reminding us of how appreciative the hotel was for our business, and asking if there was anything we'd need to make our stay more enjoyable. When it was time to get our bags out of the car, no one pointed us to a rickety dolly to pile our own bags on and wheel them to our room. A bellman took care of all that for us. The service was top-shelf for our entire stay. The staff was constantly seeking ways to delight us. The meals were excellent. The pool and suite were immaculate. I will remember every detail of our time there. We could have chosen a Hyatt and had a nice, clean place to sleep. But it would not have been the luxurious, once-in-a-lifetime experience that we enjoyed and are still talking about.

There are services. And then there are experiences.

Are your products and services the Four Seasons of your industry? If not, let's step them up.

Take Action

Before you move on to the next chapter, do this:

- Decide what your free and paid offers are.

- Take your offer to the next level in some UnCloned way.

- Think through your offer's value and everything it includes so you can convey that in your sales copy, marketing campaign assets, and when it's time to sell.

CHAPTER SIX
LEAD GENERATION STRATEGY

Once you have amazing free and paid offers, you need to get eyeballs on them. This is lead generation.

By my definition, lead generation is how you magnetically attract your ideal clients using creative, UnCloned, and compelling communication and marketing strategies. Before your brain explodes trying to figure out what that means, let me break it down a bit further:

Lead generation is the strategy for driving traffic to whatever you're selling.

There are a number of ways to do this, ranging from low- to high-tech and inexpensive to pricey. But before we dive into what those methods are and how to put them into action, I want you to understand some very important things:

1. **Lead generation is not a step you can skip if you actually want to make sales.**

2. **Lead generation is going to cost you.**

3. **Lead generation requires people.**

4. **Lead generation means you think about getting those people before you think about their money.**

It's easy to think that if your free and paid offers are dope enough, everyone will just find them and flock to them. But if it were that simple, business owners wouldn't struggle with sales. Gone are the days when you can throw up a social media post announcing your new thing, sit back, and wait for the flood of payment notifications.

We are in an attention economy. Every business out there is fighting—and buying—attention. Your potential customers are being marketed to all day, every day. They have a lot of options to choose from. It's competitive out here, which means you'll have to play to win, deliberately and consistent-ly. Bringing leads into your business is an intentional process of bringing people to you and your thing. So lead generation requires you to get in the game, if you want to capture peo-ple's attention.

As with everything else in business, lead generation is also an investment of time and some money. Depending on which lead generation strategies you decide are best for your campaign, you may need to learn how to use a new software or do some digging to learn more about your target audi-ence and where to find them. You may need to spend money on ads, tech tools, or building out a funnel. You'll be putting some work and spending money in the process. Be prepared.

In addition to some elbow grease and a credit card, you'll also need people. You may have your own audience already, but your goal may be to get in front of even more people. You may be starting from ground zero with no audience, so you are on a mission to generate leads to build an audience from scratch. The extent of your reach and the size of your platform, which includes your social media followings and email list, or the relationships to leverage someone else's, directly determines how profitable your offer will be. Whether you are selling something or generating leads to grow your following or launch a podcast, the point is that your offer cannot be profitable or successful without people. *Period.*

Typically, once an offer is created, an entrepreneur's next thought is getting to the money. If that has been you since you finished the last chapter and created your UnCloned offers, slow down, cowpoke. We have to get the people in the door first.

I consult with small business owners all the time who start calculating potential revenue before putting effective lead strategies in place. We work together to create these incredible, UnCloned offers and before I can even part my lips to talk about how we're going to drive traffic to that offer, they want to jump right to sales. And while profitability should be a priority—and I am here for it—I have to bring them back to this step. We cannot put, as our elders say, the cart before the horse. When it comes to profitability, you have to put people before money.

These are strategies designed to get you more—say it with me—*eyeballs*, on your offer.

The lead generation strategy that you choose, whether you are striving to reach a wide pool of people or targeting a smaller, strategic segment of the market, matters. The more attention you can grab from your ideal audience, the more profitable it will be.

Let's talk about how you'll make that happen.

KNOW YOURSELF

There are a lot of variables when it comes to lead generation strategies and choosing which one is right for you and your business. There is no one-size-fits-all-solution, and you'll be doing some experimenting to finally figure out which approaches work for you. And your choices may change as you change, your business scales, and the goals for your marketing campaigns shift.

But here are a few things to consider as you are determining which lead generation strategies are best for you:

Your budget. Access to capital is a factor. You know your business bank account, so before you jump into choosing and developing your lead generation strategy, you want to be clear on how much you have to invest. Ad campaigns and high-tech strategies can be costly, while shooting out a few direct messages, a low-tech strategy, can be done for free. So you'll want to consider costs when choosing your strategies.

Your tech-savviness. Do you know how to use a funnel? How comfortable are you with webinar software and technology? If you haven't mastered any of this, these are things that you can learn, BUT, you have to be committed to the cause. If you find learning new technology frustrating, you don't have the time to play with it, or the money to hire support, you may be more comfortable with strategies that do not require a lot of tech.

Your people preference and personality. Do you prefer to sell to one person at a time or do you prefer a one-to-many approach, like a webinar, virtual conference, or speaking? Knowing how you like to interact with people is important. There are strategies that are more touchy-feely, and those that will allow you to market to the masses from a platform.

You'll want to decide which route works best for you.

Your offer's price. Pricing is also a driver. If your offer is free or a low cost, it would probably not make sense (or cents) for you to point those people to schedule a 1:1 call with you. But to sell a $25,000 mastermind, those 1:1 calls could potentially be much more profitable, and therefore, worth your time. Consider your offer's value and your bandwidth before you settle on your lead generation strategy.

INBOUND VS. OUTBOUND TRAFFIC STRATEGIES

There are two types of lead generation strategies: inbound and outbound.

Inbound lead generation is creating content and campaigns that bring in website visitors and converts them into leads. Inbound traffic strategies make your brand more discoverable online, in search engines, and on social media platforms. By creating, publishing, and promoting valuable content, engage visitors in an information exchange. You give them something valuable and sexy, and in return, they pay you with their contact information with a promise to allow you to continue the conversation by email, text, or some other means.

A quick note here: When it comes to what you give in exchange for someone's information, keep in mind that it does not have to be free, and it should never, ever, be trash.

Yes, we talked about free offers in the last chapter and why you need one. But I want you to focus more on value and creativity, as opposed to the easiest, cheapest thing you can think of to give away. Instead of giving your bare minimum, go harder.

You could have someone opt-in for a premium pricing guide. Or a free ticket to an event or a live experience. Your free offer could be a resource that is really going to improve somebody's life that you package and present as a checklist. Whatever you choose, make it something that speaks to value of your business, represents your brand well, and gets your audience hyped to have it.

Keep in mind that giving away something for free isn't the cakewalk it used to be. In general, people are a lot more protective of their time and their inboxes. So they only stop and pay attention to offers that interest and intrigue them. A quality free offer not only increases the likelihood of engaging your audience at a higher rate, but, once again, sets you apart from the crowd.

Your peers are throwing that tired "freebie" out there, shouting "gimmie" the loudest, and wondering why they are not generating quality leads or converting sales. But that is not you. We're UnCloned, right? Right. So think outside the box. Do what your competitors won't, and you'll collect the money they don't.

Now let's get back to our regularly scheduled programming.

Inbound lead generation strategies are 90 percent of what you see used online. Common types of inbound lead generation strategies include:

Social Media (This could be paid traffic, such as ads or sponsored posts, on Facebook, Instagram, Google, or any other platform that offers advertisements.)

- Social Media Partnerships (This could be streaming from someone else's platform, such as a private Facebook group.)

- Media, Press, and Public Relations

- Affiliate Partners

- Brand Ambassadors

- Live Streaming

- Speaking

- Vending at Local Events

- Your existing clients

You have probably seen these strategies at play online at some point. They are commonly used, but typically in basic and lackluster ways. The key to making these lead generation strategies pop is to UnClone them and make whatever strategy you use your own.

For example, I recently spoke at a very popular business conference for women entrepreneurs in Atlanta. That month, I created a lead generation campaign to drive traffic to my free UnCloned Tribe app. So I decided to devise a creative way to make the most out of both.

I took the audio recording of the talk I gave and uploaded it to the app. Then, I created Instagram and Facebook posts promoting the talk, telling my followers they could listen to the talk for free by downloading the app. The strategy was a hit and cost me nothing but a little time. Now once all of my new app subscribers enter my UnCloned world, I can introduce them to my books and digital products. And then my memberships. And then my higher-end services such as my mastermind and VIP Days.

Do you see where I am going with this?

Effective lead generation is about creativity and strategy. I could have given this awesome talk to the fifty or so ladies who caught it live in the room and been done with it. Speaking box checked. Or I could have thrown a link to my talk up on my Facebook page and said, "Hey, guys! I gave this really great talk that you should go check out if you feel like it!" Had I done either of those, I would have limited myself to just one lead generation opportunity versus two, and had I not drove traffic to my app, I would have had no way of tracking who took action and watched the talk. Lastly, I would not have had access to those people to be able to market to them again in the future. I gave them something of value—access to a replay of my talk—in exchange for all their contact information, which is required to subscribe to the app.

A little creativity goes a long way. As you think about which lead generation strategy to choose, always give some thought to how you can remix it in a creative way that meets your goals, makes the most of your content, and gets you access to people who are legitimately interested in your offer.

THE PROS AND CONS OF INBOUND MARKETING

There are pluses and minuses to everything in business, and marketing is no exception. Let's talk about the pros and cons of inbound marketing.

Here's the upside to inbound marketing:

Less research intensive. Once you are clear on who you are marketing to and which strategy is the best fit for you, the rest is execution. In most instances, you won't have to dig for a lot of data.

Easy to automate. For most inbound marketing strategies, there is a way to automate some aspect of it. Once you set up an ad campaign, for example, it will run on its own while you watch your analytics and tweak accordingly. Brand ambassador and affiliate programs can also be run through an automated funnel, so you can minimize your manual labor with those too. You can put tech to work for you to make the process and implementation easier.

Broader reach. As a result of the tech options and access to automation, you can reach more people easier.

And here's the downside to inbound marketing:

Higher Costs. There are costs associated with technology, software, paid advertising, and even media if you decide to hire a public relations professional to help you with media placements.

Less control over who comes into your world. Inbound marketing is like casting a net in the ocean, catching a ton of different types of fish, and after choosing which ones are tasty to you from the bunch, you let the others just hang out and play amongst themselves.

If you are marketing to the masses, you will get all types of people coming into your offers and community. Some will be active participants in your free Facebook group, some won't. Some will buy paid products and services, and some won't. Some will buy offers and do the work required to succeed, some won't. Some will love what you do, and some won't, but still stay just to peep your game.

So if you want a more exclusive audience, you may want to give some thought to outbound lead generation strategies to get in front of those people in a targeted way.

Outbound lead generation strategies are used to pitch someone who isn't expecting it, also known as cold pitching. This is a tactic that is commonly used for high-ticket sales and is ideal when you want to connect, communicate, and position yourself for a collaboration with very specific clients, companies, brands, and events.

Outbound lead generation strategies include:

- Direct Mail

- Email Marketing

- Direct Email

- Invite-only events

One of my most successful outbound lead generation outcomes to date has been a targeted outreach to conferences and events coordinators who cater to my ideal clients. Once I compiled a short list of events that I determined to be a good fit, I put a customized email together for each one. My pitch: to give free copies of my book to their VIP event attendees. In addition to a brief description of my book, along with links to my Amazon Author Page, I also included my professionally designed media kit so the person who I was pitching to could see that I was the real deal.

Each time I've tested this, it worked like gangbusters. Quality events are always looking for free swag to upgrade their attendees' experience, and it's well worth the investment for me. For a few dollars to cover the cost of printing and ordering my books, I can generate some new, qualified leads—who, because they'd paid for a higher level of access for the event, were my type of people—and boost my authority and credibility. In a scenario like this, running an ad or DMing someone would not have yielded the same result. Outbound lead generation has a more personal touch and is viewed as more professional when you're seeking to establish B2B partnerships or relationships with premium clients.

THE PROS AND CONS OF OUTBOUND MARKETING

There are some great advantages to outbound lead generation, and some possible pitfalls too. Here are some quick thoughts on both.

First, the upside:

Exclusivity. In these scenarios, you are highly focused on a small subset of the market. You are cherry-picking people who you want to work with as opposed to bringing in all types of folks. Depending on your product or service, you may fare better with a small group, particularly when they are purchasing a premium service. If you are selling a high-ticket program, such as a mastermind, you may have very specific requirements for participating. Hand-picking the people who you want to bring into the program can increase the likelihood of success for you and them.

And the biggest downside:

No automation. Creating your outreach emails and pitches, and then getting them in the right hands, is typically a manual process. First, you'll have to do some extensive research to determine who you want to connect with and the best way to contact them. Then, you will be reaching out to your leads directly, usually one at a time. This can be tedious, so these strategies will require a little more time to work them effectively.

LOW-TECH VS. HIGH-TECH

LEAD GENERATION STRATEGIES

When it comes to marketing, particularly online, technology is one of the biggest barriers to entry. Most business owners have a love/hate relationship with tech. You've probably guessed that I am a proclaimed geek when it comes to new tools, software, and gadgets. I *live* to tinker with tech, so I tend to use a lot of high-tech lead generation strategies in my marketing campaigns. But I know from working closely with a broad range of business owners that everyone is not anxiously awaiting the next new thing to play with. In fact, there are far more people who are anti-tech than there are tech enthusiasts.

But whether you love tech or hate it with a passion, fortunately, you have options when it comes to using it to bring in more leads.

Low-tech marketing strategies use the least amount of tech possible to attract leads.

Here's the upside to low-tech strategies:

Leverage what you already have. By now, I am sure you have at least Facebook and Instagram pages, and you may be active on other platforms as well, depending on the nature of your business. That is really all you need to get started with this. You don't need a lot of fancy tools or a lot of money, so you can get going right away.

Short learning curve. Low-tech strategies are easy to learn. You won't spend a lot of time reading and researching how to get these strategies to work. They are as easy as 1-2-3.

Fast results. Low-tech strategies are ideal when you want to get clients and customers right now. Since you don't need much to get started, you can hit the ground running quickly.

If there is a downside to using low-tech strategies, it would be the lack of automation. You aren't using funnels and sequences here. All that means is you'll have to work a little harder to get to people, and that's okay. I would rather you invest more sweat equity than to sit on the sidelines and miss out on the opportunity to get in front of people and sell. So if you decide that low-tech is where you want to start with generating leads, let's get to it!

Here are some low-tech strategies for you to consider:

Social Selling is using compelling and creative marketing to get people to take action via social media. Social media is a fairly easy tool to use. You don't have to get super techy with bots and other automated tools. Instead, you can get right into people's inbox.

One of the ways to UnClone social selling is to leverage the direct message, culturally and socially known as "The DM." While people commonly use DMs for personal communication, for some customers, it is still unexpected for a business to contact them with a personal message.

If sliding into the DM can be effective when shooting your shot with a potential new boo, then it can work for introducing yourself to a potential new client. The same rules apply: get a cute pic, say, "Hey", introduce yourself, and ask if it's okay to give them a call sometime to get to know them better.

Almost every social media platform—Facebook, Instagram, LinkedIn—has a direct message or private message feature. To leverage them to easily skyrocket your sales, send a direct message to leads with a cute photo—say of you or you working side-by-side with a client—or a great introductory video along with one of the following:

• A request to DM you back to continue the conversation.

- A phone number to reach you for a consultation, via call or text.

- A link to a checkout page to purchase your offer, or a link to your website to learn more about your products or services.

You could also run this same strategy with Instagram and Facebook stories, IGTV, and YouTube. Share your videos straight to people's DMs. Whichever option you choose, add a creative caption as a soft pitch to tell them a little about you and what you do, and send.

This approach is friendly, personable, and most importantly distinct. It's unlikely that your potential clients and customers are getting a lot of businesses who are messaging them directly, particularly in a non-pushy, sales-ey, way.

GETTING UP CLOSE AND PERSONAL OUTSIDE OF SOCIAL

Aside from social selling, you can get in front of more people with these low-tech strategies:

- **1-on-1 Calls.** Calls are a tried-and-true sales strategy for businesses, large and small. If you run a call right, you can sell something from $.01 to $1,000,000, just by getting on the phone.

- **Meetups.** Meeting with people never gets old. A lot of deals are closed in person.

- **Audits and Assessments.** These are great tools for helping people to see what holes they have in their lives and in businesses, and how what you offer can help fill them. Typically you see these used online, but why not UnClone it and meet with people face-to-face to walk through them and answer questions right on the spot?

- **Networking and Speaking with Lead Capturing Systems.** Whenever you are in a networking setting or speaking at an event, you have an opportunity to generate leads. You can use any of the following tools to help you:

  - **Jotform on Mobile Phone/Laptop.** Jotform is a software that allows you to create questionnaires and other forms online. You can create yours and bookmark it on your mobile phone or laptop. When you are at a networking event, you can whip out your form, have people complete it, and now you have a growing database of leads.

  - **Rip Cards.** Rip Cards are a piece of printed marketing collateral that I absolutely love, and I keep a bag full whenever I am at an event. These are perforated, so you want to print a short blurb or bio about yourself at the top—along with a link to your website or offer—and then have your leads fill out the bottom portion with their contact information. When they finish, you rip off the portion with their information, and they keep the top half.

You can have a graphic designer create these for you, or if you're in the mood for a little DIY, I have a dope rip card template that you can create right in Canva available in my online shop. **Check it out at https://audriarichmond. shop/.**

- **URL to Checkout Form.** Once you've had a conversation with someone and they are ready to purchase, leave them with a link right to your offer's checkout page.

- **Good 'Ol Pen and Paper.** We never miss an opportunity to collect leads, okay? So when all else fails, pull out a pen and a sheet of paper. Ask for names, emails, and social media handles, and pass it around the room.

High-tech lead generation strategies use a very high level and strategic amount of technology and marketing automation to attract leads and customers to your offer. Technology can be intimidating, but if you love systems and processes, you'll love the automation aspect of strategies such as webinars and challenges. When you leverage automation, you can reach twice as many people as you would without technology. So while these strategies are a little more complicated to execute, the results are worth it.

Here are some more positives of high-tech strategies:

Set you apart. Due to the complicated and sometimes costly nature of high-tech strategies, a lot of your competitors stay away from them. So when you come onto the scene with a beautifully produced live stream or virtual event, you will immediately stand out.

Make you look like a pro. This level of strategy is not for beginners. When you see high-tech lead generation done right, it puts the business in a different category in the eyes of the consumer. People know investment and quality when they see it.

It's evergreen. Once you create a video series, webinar, or funnel, you can set it and forget it, unless you decide to update the content or offer.

You could save some money in the long run. What I love about virtual events is the ease—once you get over the tech hump—and the potentially reduced costs associated with the event. Yes, you will spend money in production, but you may save on the cost of a venue, vendors, travel, and other logistics. Consider this trade-off.

And as far as the downside:

Expensive to produce. High-tech strategies usually require a decent budget, particularly if you need to buy software, equipment, or hire someone to help you. We're not talking about turning your office into a blockbuster movie set, but you will need some quality tools. So you will need access to some revenue.

Steeper learning curve. Tech takes time to learn and get right. It will take some time to understand the various tools out there, what their features are, and how to use them.

Complexity. Challenges and virtual events may look simple, but they really are not. We are not talking about you waking up and hopping on a Zoom to talk for an hour. These are full-blown productions. With challenges, for example, there are different components and agendas for each day. Each day has a different call to action. There are a lot of fun, moving parts to these strategies, especially if you want to make them UnCloned.

Some high-tech strategies to consider are:

- Challenges

- Video Series

- Webinars

- Events

- Partnerships and Collaborations

- Evergreen Funnels

- Virtual Conferences

- Virtual Breakout Sessions at Events

FOR GOODNESS SAKES, JUST TRY IT

Now for some real, real talk.

I've hopefully given you some good insight into the many options you have for generating leads. As you are considering which strategies to jump into for your campaign, I want to urge you to do something.

Don't overthink. Just choose. Just try.

Marketing is very much a trial-and-error sort of thing. Even with all the insight and information I am sharing in this book, there is still much for you to experience and experiment with on your own. My job is to tell you what I know—but your job is to take what I tell you and run with it. Take some risks. Mess some stuff up. See what works. It's all part of the process.

As you try more things, you'll learn what works for your audience, what excites them more, and what, in turn, drives more engagement.

You'll learn more about yourself and what you can do that you never thought you could. You'll surprise yourself and become a tech guru. Or you will find out that you thought you would love livestreaming, but what really makes your heart skip a beat is getting in front of people, speaking at live events, and gathering leads that way. But you will not know until you try.

I know it's scary. Spending your hard-earned money on ads that you may not get back is scary. Sitting down and tinkering with technology that you've never seen before is scary. Doing something that you've never done before is scary. But embracing that fear, feeling it, and facing it, is a must.

You picked up this book to learn how to grow, how to stretch, so damnit, let's do it.

You may put the eBook out there, and nobody downloads it. You may have to tweak the format, or the ad copy, or the call to action, but whatever you do, don't give up on anything too easily—especially not yourself.

Take Action

Before you move on to the next chapter, do this:

- Decide which inbound or outbound lead generation strategies are the best fit for your personality, budget, offer, and the people that you are seeking to reach.

- Decide how comfortable you are with playing with some new technology, and, if so, which high-tech lead generation strategies you can incorporate into your campaign.

- If technology is not your thing, choose a low-tech lead generation strategy to use.

"When it comes to what you give in exchange for someone's information, keep in mind that it does not have to be free, and it should never, ever, be trash."

- Audria Richmond

CHAPTER SEVEN
THE MARKETING PLAN

Every profitable marketing campaign needs a plan, specifically a marketing plan. A marketing plan is a detailed summary of all the key pieces of your campaign.

When you are planning a campaign, you should think of your marketing plan as your can't-live-without-it guide. Every aspect of your campaign should be included, from A to Z. It should be comprehensive, clear, and compiled in such a way that anyone in your company or on your team could pick up the ball and run with it. When your marketing plan is done right, someone who has rolled with you for twenty years or an employee who just started yesterday can take it and know exactly what needs to happen to bring your full marketing campaign to life, flawlessly.

Every winning team has a playbook. Regardless of what the sport is—football, basketball, hockey—each coach creates a playbook to lay out how the team moves and runs the ball or the puck. The playbook is about precision and accuracy. It tells everyone where to be and what to do to win. The playbook keeps the team on course, eliminates guesswork, and ensures that if any one of the players, or the coach herself, falls off the face of the earth, the team can keep playing. The engine keeps running. Experienced teams swear by the playbook, and you will not catch a real, professional sports organization without one.

This is the mindset that I want you to adopt too.

In your mind, your marketing campaign may be simple. But I can assure you it's not. Even if the goal of your campaign is to sell ten new products for your first launch, you aren't just going to stand on the corner and beg everyone who walks by to buy something. This may work for some cute Girl Scouts, but you are probably a little older and you need a more sophisticated plan, homie.

The bottom line is whether your campaign is super simple or super complex, you have several steps to take to make it happen. Your marketing plan keeps your campaign—and you—together. How does it help you? I am so glad you asked.

A marketing plan:

Guides the entire process. If there is a word that summed up a marketing plan, it would be details. I can tell you right now, I am going to pick your brain to pieces and *detail you to death* in this chapter. You may hate me now, but, if you stick it out and see this through, you will thank me later. As someone who has launched more times than I can count, I can tell you that a campaign is not something you want to wing. When you have a plan, you have a guide to prevent you from making mistakes, wasting time and money, and losing sight of your goals.

Keeps you accountable. Once you see your goals all pretty and laid out in front of you, it will be hard to ignore them. Your marketing plan should put the fire under your behind to stick to your schedule and follow through on your tasks to get this campaign going.

Tracks your results. A well-developed plan will be sure you capture everything you need to know about your marketing campaign. It will show you what worked and what didn't so you have some real data and metrics to determine what flopped and what was successful. With that intel, you will know if you should trash your campaign, tweak it, or rinse-and-repeat next time.

Your marketing plan is all about details. The good news is that the work you've done in the previous chapters of this book has all led to this.

All the key decisions you've made so far—solidifying your authority and credibility, crafting your offer, and choosing your lead generation strategies—feed into your marketing plan. You've done a lot of the hard work, figured a lot of stuff out, and you are bringing all those pieces together into one document that tells you—and your team—everything you need to know to make this marketing campaign the most epic event your business has ever seen.

TYPES OF MARKETING CAMPAIGNS

The next decision you need to make is the reason for your marketing campaign. Marketing campaigns are built for one of two reasons—to launch a new product, service, or offer or relaunch an existing offer.

If you are launching a new offer, keep in mind the time, energy, and funds it takes to pull a campaign off from start to finish. So before you jump into this, you want to ask—and answer—two key questions:

1. Is this something that people actually want?

2. What authority and credibility have I established around this new product or service? (In other words, have I proven that I can deliver what I am offering?)

The last thing you want to do is sweat out your deodorant to make this campaign work, only to find out that nobody wants your offer. Or you are unable to sell it because no one knows who you are, or you are selling something brand new, and your audience is completely confused. Make sure you've done the research first to validate your idea and that you've done the necessary work to be sure your people know and accept you as someone they believe in and want to buy from.

On the flip, this could be an offer you've put out there before. There are a number of reasons why you would relaunch an existing offer:

- You've decided to turn a former free offer into a paid offer.

- You could have added some new features or more value to a program or product, and you are rereleasing the new and improved version.

- You want to position a current product in a bigger or different way.

- You want to increase enrollment in a program.

- You are targeting a new audience.

THE COMPONENTS OF A MARKETING PLAN

Before we break down what your marketing plan should include, please pause for an announcement.

**************This is the Emergency Broadcast System With a Special Announcement for The One-Man and One-Woman Shows (AKA The Entrepreneurs Doing All of This S%#T By Themselves)**********

As you start to read through this, I know you will be wondering why a document of this magnitude is needed. Yes, this is something that bigger companies do. And that's exactly why I want you to do it.

You won't be alone forever. You will be scaling your business. You will have a marketing team supporting you. But if you continue to think small, you will stay small. Start thinking and acting big now.

I can say that one of the mindset shifts that catapulted me into the big leagues—even before I actually got there—was thinking beyond where I was and preparing for where I wanted to be.

When I started strategizing, creating, planning, and implementing like a big company, I started showing up differently, and my profits reflected it. I run the backend of my company as if I have a team of twenty and a multi-million dollar agency because one day soon, it will be.

You have to start doing the same.

Now back to our regularly scheduled programming.

You can capture the information for your marketing plan in any way you choose. Grab a notebook and write it out by hand. Type it out and print it. Or you can purchase my Launch Planner, which I developed exactly for this purpose. I'll let you choose which method you liked to use, as long as you choose one.

The point of putting in this work is to have your plan out of your head and on paper. You want to be able to see it all laid out, share it with others as needed, and refer back to it throughout your campaign.

Once you're ready to map it out, here are the **20 Things That Every Marketing Plan Should Have:**

1. **Purpose of Your Campaign.** You want to be clear on the intent and inspiration behind your campaign. Why are you launching or relaunching this offer? Are you seeking to get new clients and customers? Are you seeking to build your authority and credibility? If you are running a nonprofit, are you setting out to increase volunteers or to make a difference in your community in a big way? Know what your campaign is about and what you are here to do with it.

2. **Your Idea.** What is your idea or concept? For example, when I created the UnCloned Marketing Membership, I wanted a community for business owners to learn proven marketing strategies that increased their profitability. Once I was clear on my idea, I could move into the details of what that would look like. You want to flesh out your idea and be certain that it makes sense for the market.

3. **Your Mission, Vision, and Why.** Next, you'll want to define your mission, vision, and why. You've thought about your purpose, but go deeper and detail your vision for

impacting your audience and why it's important to you and them.

4. **What Success Would Look Like for You.** If you could waive a marketing magic wand and have the most successful campaign ever, what would that look like for you? Would it be to make money? Would it be to have new people subscribe to your newsletter? Are you looking to step up your authority and credibility factor in your industry? These are the types of results you are looking for. List them out and include them in your plan.

5. **Goals and Objectives.** Keep going with your key goals and objectives. How will you know that your campaign is successful? How much money will you have made or how many new followers will you have? Get specific so you know what results you are looking for.

6. **Target Audience/Target Situation™.** If you have an established business, and this is not your first time launching this offer, you want to document who your target audience is. But if this is your first time giving this a try, you may not know exactly who your audience is, but you may know the situation they are struggling with and how your product or services is a fix for their issue. That is your target situation. You want to document which of the two is the focus for your particular campaign.

7. **How You Plan to Test Your Idea and Market Research.** In this section of your plan, you want to document the process you will use to determine if the market wants what you offer, before you jump into a full-blown, time

consuming marketing campaign. How will you beta test your offer and see if it piques some interest first?

8. **Type of Paid Offer.** Are you launching a product, service, event, or a combination of all of these?

9. **Details and Summary of Your Paid Offer.** This is where you get into the specifics of your offer.

   If you were explaining your offer to your customer, what would you tell them? What would you include in the product description for a catalog or your sales page? Write everything the offer includes, what the features and benefits are, and the value each of those provides. Anticipate every question your customer may ask about your product or service, and answer them here.

10. **How You Plan to Wow and Onboard Your New Clients.** This is the detailed process that lays out what happens once someone decides to take the action you want them to take. Do they receive a welcome email or gift? Are you calling each person to thank them?

11. **Type of Free Offer (AKA Lead Magnet).** Write out the details of your free offer. What is it? What does it include? How will people access it?

12. **Traffic and Promotion Strategy.** Go back to your notes on your lead generation strategy. Document how you will be driving traffic to your free offer. What process will you use to convert leads from your free offer to your paid offer, or the next step you want them to take, like signing up for a group or coming out to be a part of a fundrais-

ing walk or run? If you are running ads, include that. If you are planning to livestream 10 times in a week, include that too. Have a plan for every platform you intend to promote on.

13. **Launch Dates.** This section will be your master calendar and schedule. In addition to the date you will officially launch your offer, you want to document your other key dates as well. Those dates could include when you will need to have each of your promotions designed and ready to go, when your videos will be recorded, or meetings with your launch team. Put all your dates in one place so you have them at a glance.

14. **Snapshot and Audit of Your Numbers Before the Launch.** Know your numbers so you have some data and metrics to compare at the end of your launch. How many social media followers did you have? How many subscribers did you have on your newsletter or podcast? How many products had you sold this time last year? With this type of information, you'll be able to better analyze your campaign to determine if it was effective or not.

15. **List of Top Promotional Activities.** This is the fun part. Decide what you will be giving away to promote your offer. Are you printing special t-shirts for you and your team? Mailing your attendees branded popcorn to munch on while watching your video series? Giving out discounts for a limited-collection bracelet sold at your boutique? Think about all the creative ways to get the word out about your launch.

16. **Assets for Each Phase of the Launch.** Plan out all the assets you'll need for your launch. Think about this in terms of phases and what you need for each one. If you are recording a promotional video, you may need a slide deck and the actual video. For your free offer, you'll probably have some sort of web page for people to opt-in and download the freebie, so you need the page and the freebie too. You may need a special shop for your products if you are selling them online, or new signage for your store if you have a brick-and-mortar location. So you want to detail out everything you need to completely execute your campaign.

17. **Production Team and Budget Needed.** If you plan to hire people to help you with your campaign, list out the roles you'd like to hire for. I'll talk about who you should consider for your launch team later in this chapter.

    Know your numbers when it comes to money. You don't want to be in a situation where you are halfway through your launch and you get hit with some unexpected cost. You should have a budget sheet and a line item for every expense associated with your launch.

18. **Schedule of Dates for All Promotional Activities.** Honing in on your promotional phase, list out all of the dates for your activities. When are you mailing out gifts or coupons?

19. **How You Plan to Track All Sales.** You have to track your sales so you know what's coming in. You can use an Excel spreadsheet or some other tool. Or you can check out my

sales tracker to make it simple for you at **https://audri-arichmond.shop/.**

20. **How You Plan to Track All Launch Activities.** This is where you track every activity of your launch, including the date you will release it and metrics for success. For example, if I am hosting a virtual conference and giving every person who registers a link to download a digital badge with their picture on it so they can share it on social, I'll want to list that activity out and how I will know how effective that strategy was. I may be tracking shares or downloads from my site. This is the type of information you want to capture here.

MAKE IT LOOK GOOD, PLEASE

You are playing in the major leagues now, and after all of this work to plan out an incredible campaign, you don't want to kill it with whack graphics. You want people to see anything associated with your campaign, and your brand overall, and immediately think quality and professional. People will make a decision whether or not to buy from you based on how your offer is visually presented. You wouldn't expect a restaurant to serve a $100 steak on a paper plate, would you? So you don't want to sell your offer wrapped in ugly, raggedy packaging.

Deciding how you will brand your campaign is totally up to you when it comes to the creative. If you have a brand identity already—that would be your logo, colors, and design elements—you can follow your branding style guide and create assets that are consistent with that. Or you can have some fun and create a new theme that is specific to your campaign. Consider what you are offering and how you want people to feel when they experience it. When you see my branding, it is always bright and bold because I want people to immediately feel energetic and associate my brand with high creativity and the unexpected. So you want to identify the vibe of your campaign and convey that through the aesthetics.

You may have a lot of assets to create or a few, depending on the simplicity or complexity of your campaign, and whether you are marketing online, offline, or both. Here are some assets you may want to consider:

- Logo

- Packaging or Product Branding

- Print or social media flyers

- Countdown Graphics to post on social media leading up to your launch

- Livestream graphic (This displays while people are waiting for your livestream to start.)

- Instagram Story Graphics

- Facebook Story Graphics

- Cover for Your Facebook Business Page

- Badges (These are cool for virtual events or challenges; everyone who registers for the event or signs up for the challenge can get one to share on social and drum up promotion for your campaign.)

- Ad graphics

- Email headers

- Workbooks, Checklists, or other templates to support your offer

- Custom Slide Decks

BUILDING YOUR LAUNCH TEAM

We're going big, right? That means you can't do all of this alone. You need a marketing launch team. These are pros who will support you with the major moving parts of your campaign, and, let's be honest, keep you from snatching your hair out at the root. Launching can be stressful, and the more tasks you can outsource, the better. But while support is great, one of the biggest mistakes you can make is hiring before you are ready.

You don't want to hire a team for any of the following reasons:

You don't want to learn anything new. Laziness or fear are not excuses here. Before you outsource anything, you should have some idea of what it takes to do it yourself. Familiarize yourself with the process so at least you can have an informed conversation with a professional and not get robbed out of ignorance. If you sit your butt down in the chair and learn some new skills, you may find that what you are afraid to do is not as hard as you thought.

You don't want to do anything yourself. If you have the skillset, use it. My home office doubles as a DIY video studio so I do not have to pay someone. I am a professional graphic designer, and while I don't design as much as I used to for clients, I will get into Adobe Illustrator when I need to and get busy. It takes a little more time, but I save thousands of dollars a year that I can allocate towards other things in my business.

There will be plenty of things to spend money on, so use your resources wisely. If you have a limited budget, you are better off saving coins to use for other expenses. If you have a pro-level skillset—and the time—put it to work.

If and when you decide to bring a team onboard, here are the people you'll want on your squad:

- **Photographer.** You will need professional images to brand your offer, websites, and marketing assets. You may have images of yourself, models, or stock images, but they should all be quality and professional. No selfies, please.

- **Videographer.** If you will be using videos for your campaign, hire a professional to ensure they are high-quality.

- **Graphic and Website Designer.** Your campaign will need some graphic bling. Websites, landing pages, and graphics for your promotions, at a bare minimum. The more elaborate your campaign is, the more assets you'll need. If you aren't a designer, consider hiring someone to help.

- **Copywriter.** Like graphics, copy is an essential part of any marketing campaign. You'll possibly need ad copy, emails, web copy, and copy for any direct mail pieces you create. Bringing someone onboard who specializes in ad copy is a smart investment, if you can swing it.

- **Social Media Pro/Specialist.** This should be someone who understands the ins and outs of social media. If you are absolutely adamant about not messing with social media yourself, get the help you need. Professionals can help with everything from mapping out a content strategy for your campaign to actually managing your accounts and performing analysis.

- **Tech and Marketing Automation Pro.** If you know that you struggle with tech, and you decide that a high-tech launch is best for you, bring in a pro. I would rather see you learn these skills on your own, but maybe you just don't have the time or the bandwidth. If this is something that you can pay someone to take off your plate so that you can focus on the rest of your campaign, do it.

Take Action

Before you move on to the next chapter, do this:

- Get clear on what type of marketing campaign you are creating. Is this a new offer or a relaunch of an existing offer?

- Sit your butt in a chair, get some caffeine, and write that marketing plan alllllll the way out.

- Decide if you need a launch team, who you will need to hire, and make a list of vendors to fill those slots.

CHAPTER EIGHT
LAUNCHING AND SALES

A launch is the series of sequential events or experiences to bring your potential client into your campaign. This is where you put your marketing campaign into action, from promotion to paid offer.

Now I am not going to BS you—launching is hard. But the beauty of it is that it's a rinse-and-repeat process that, once you master it, you can use over and over again. And it gets easier every time.

You may be gasping for air even as you get to this chapter, realizing how much goes into building a marketing campaign. You are right, it's a lot of work, but launching is also incredibly rewarding. Launching is where you see all your hard work come together. You have the perfect offer. You know how you are going to get eyeballs on that offer. You've planned everything out and documented all your details in your marketing plan so that nothing falls through the cracks. And now it's show time.

Up until this point, you've been so focused on the excitement of it all—putting your thing out there, the packed-out promotions, and, of course, the profits, if sales is one of your goals. You have only thought about the victory and how everything will work out perfectly as planned. In your mind, this is the greatest thing you've ever done or created, and the whole world is going to see it and fall in love with it as much as you have. You'll have the whole town tossing you up in the air on their shoulders like the little boy on the Old El Paso taco kit commercial. Confetti is shooting out of a cannon. The champagne is flowing. The whole world is celebrating you, cheering for you, and checking for you.

You've been all smiles until it's time to step out onto the stage and do the thing.

Cue the stage fright.

This is usually the part when the nerves start to kick in. You're afraid. You're doubting that you can pull this off. You want to crawl back under your desk and hide.

These feelings may be temporary and you get right back to I-got-this mode. Or if you're like me just a few years ago, you are questioning your whole life and you are two seconds away from pulling the plug on the whole thing. But what I want you to know that everything you are feeling is natural. Launching can be an emotional rollercoaster, up one day, down the next.

There is only one cure for that sick-tummy feeling you have right now—get your mind right. If you have a messed-up mindset, your launch is doomed to flop before you can get it off the ground. So I am here to help.

C'mon, boo. I got you.

YOUR LAUNCH MINDSET

Over the years, I've learned that energy is a real thing.

I am no spiritual guru, but I believe your emotional state, and what you allow to infiltrate your mind and your space, influences everything. What is happening in and around you will play a part in your results and the outcome of your launch.

When professional boxers are preparing for a big fight, their entire lives revolve around that one match. They are isolated from everyone except their training team. They are eating a special, restricted diet to either add or drop weight and to get in optimal condition.

Your launch is your heavyweight fight. So you want to treat it that way.

In addition to eating your vegetables, drinking your protein shakes, and pulling out that jump rope, there are a few more shifts you need to make:

Get rid of the sucky attitude. Your attitude and mood matters. If you are in a funky place mentally, it will show. You will come on camera to shoot your videos and bark through your script. Your sales calls will suck. You don't want any of that. Set the tone for your launch from the beginning. Smile a lot, especially when you are on camera, on the phone, or in front of people.

Get rid of all sucky people. If there are people in your life who drain you every time you talk to or hang out with them, avoid them during your launch. You need all your focus and energy, so you don't have any to waste. Don't deal with anyone or do anything that doesn't make you happy or distracts you while you're in launch mode. Now is the time to snooze all suckers.

Speaking of people, here is one more thing: Find other people who you can lean on. You need at least one person who can cheer you on, listen to you vent when nothing is going right—until you figure it all out a few hours later—or who will force you to take a movie break to relax a bit.

Get rid of the bad energy. I used to be a nervous wreck with every launch. I would be in tears for a week, stressing about all the balls that got dropped and the mistakes I made. Things have changed a lot, thankfully. I got my emotions in check.

Now when I launch, I do what I know how to do, technically speaking. And then energetically, I light candles. I clean up my home. I do things I love. I show up. And I let the rest unfold. I clear up all trashy energy around me and allow nothing but positivity in. And it's made a huge difference in my whole perspective, my results, and for real for real, my revenue. Money loves good energy.

Get rid of the idea that you can't fail. Yes, you read that right. Going into a launch without accepting the possibility that it could fail is the setup of all setups. I have bought failure up a few times throughout this book because it's just that important. There will be things that go right with your launch, and things that go wrong. You can bank on it. Bake it into your plan so you can be prepared and it doesn't catch you off guard. Schedules will slip. Vendors will flake. Your camera lens will crack. Stuff happens. Get used to it.

Success, to be honest, is simply starting. Success is learning a new skill or putting yourself in front of new people with some wild idea that was once just a figment of your imagination. Success is seeing this whole thing through. You are going to get some positive results out of this process. Accept the lessons and do better next time. Trust yourself, loosen up, and go along for the ride.

Get rid of comparison. I don't care who just launched the week before you or how much money they claimed they made. This is not about anyone else but you.

To be UnCloned, you have to be anti-comparison and anti-copying. You are not here to imitate, you innovate. You are not mimicking anyone else's launch goals. You are only focused on the goals that count—your own.

This is your journey. Don't trip up over your untied shoelaces trying to run your race while watching the dude next to you. If you are so busy comparing yourself to others, you'll lose excitement for what's happening in your own business.

Get rid of quitting. Whatever you do, don't quit. If you plan to run your campaign for a week, don't bail if by Wednesday, it doesn't look like you will meet your goals. See it through.

One, you want to prove to yourself that you can finish what you started. Two, you invested a lot to make this campaign happen, so don't waste your time or money. And three, until you get to the end of your campaign, you don't know what is possible.

Marketing and sales studies show—and I know this to be true from personal experience—that campaigns tend to make the most money on the first and last day of the launch. There are people who are gung ho and will jump in on Day One and others who like to procrastinate a bit, or may be waiting until they get paid to purchase.

What if the other $15,000 of your $20,000 goal is coming through on Friday at 11:59 p.m.? Is it worth the risk not to allow your launch to play all the way out? You don't want to pull the plug on your profits too soon.

Get rid of emotions. Okay, for purposes of this launch, I am going to need you to toughen up. Keep in mind, I am speaking to you as probably the most sensitive soul in the world. I was famous for taking rejection and flops personally. Every time something didn't go as planned or if someone told me no, I would be balled up, crying on my husband's shoulder, ready to give up. I got hurt whenever I got criticized, even in the slightest bit. To push through in business, I had to learn how to put my feelings in check. You have to do the same.

Business is not for the faint at heart. Launching is not for punks. The bottom line is that to get to your bottom line, you have to develop some tough skin.

This is when you have to remember who you are. You are a dope creator. A genius. An entrepreneur who was willing to try something that has never been done before. You have a good heart. And you're human. You make mistakes. So what? You also get it right a lot, too. You can't allow criticism from a stranger to make you doubt who you are or convince you to quit. NOPE. Brush your shoulders off and get back to business.

Get ready to celebrate your wins. A win is a win is a win. You may have money wins, media wins, or growth in other ways. You got people to look at your big, beautiful idea that you were brave enough to put out there. Those are all reasons to celebrate.

The Launch Pledge

Now put your hand over your heart and repeat after me.

I, [insert your name here], do solemnly swear to get—and keep—my mindset positive throughout my launch.

I will cut off all whack people, thoughts, and energy.

I will not allow fear, doubt, insecurity, or the temptation to compare or copy get the best of me.

I will not get distracted.

I accept failure as part of the process, and I will not quit on my campaign, my customers, or myself.

If I feel shaky, I will go get some fries, put my feet up, and watch my favorite movie.

Now there you go. You got this.

WHY LAUNCHES FLOP

Back to this failure thing.

There are a million and one reasons why launches flop. And it's not always your fault. As business owners, we can do it all right, have a great product, put time, energy, and money into marketing it, and the launch could still fail. It happens.

But there are some things that are within your control. Here are some classic mistakes that can almost guarantee you a failed launch:

You weren't prepared. If you don't invest enough time into planning a launch, it shows. You don't share enough information. You don't educate people enough. This is what's happened when you see someone throw up a post that says, "Hey! I have this webinar coming up! Sign up!" That's not enough conversation to get someone to give up their valuable time, much less buy something. You have to take people on a journey. Woo them a bit before you force your product or service on them.

You didn't allot enough time. If you are planning to launch for a Black Friday, you should be preparing 60-90 days out, or prepare to flop. Even if you are not launching on a holiday, you need time. Plan for a minimum of 30 days, depending on the extent of your launch and the results you are after. You cannot execute a $100K launch in three days.

Your launch is too long. Consumers get turned off with a long, complicated sale process. Know your audience, and try to keep your launch as concise as possible.

Your technology doesn't work. Have you ever been to a sales page and the buttons don't work? Or you never get a link to set an appointment for your sales call? These are things that frustrate your potential customers and can kill your launch.

You limited yourself to one medium. An UnCloned launch touches people in different ways. It's not enough to just do video—you need photos too. You need copywriting. You have to diversify your launch assets.

You have the wrong audience. You may have thousands of

147

people on your email list or following you on social media, but that doesn't mean they will buy.

You partnered with the wrong people. You may have made the mistake of thinking your partners had influence and you could leverage their audience for marketing and lead generation, only to find out they did not. Know who you are rolling with and involving in your launch.

WHAT TO TRACK DURING YOUR LAUNCH

Numbers make a lot of people uncomfortable, but you can't hide from them.

Marketing is data driven, and to ensure that your marketing is effective, you need to pay close attention to what's happening. You want to track the effectiveness of every activity during your launch.

I recommend you track the metrics below during your campaign. These may not all apply to your particular launch, but you should pick out the ones that do for each campaign you execute from here on out.

Metrics for your specific business. Depending on what your offer is, you'll want to track related metrics. So if you were selling a new toothbrush in your dental clinic, you'll be measuring the number of brushes sold. If you have a membership, then you are tracking new members, and so on.

Daily sales from your products and services. Stay on top of your money. You want to look at your sales reports at least once a day.

Social media growth and increase in followers, likes, etc. Know where you start before your campaign begins. Your marketing plan should include your numbers for all your social media platforms, and you want to track growth throughout your launch.

Call-to-Action responses. Pay attention to what you're asking people to do and if they are taking action. If at the end of your posts, you are asking people to click a link to take them to your registration page, you want to track those clicks.

Number of direct messages and social media comments and conversations. You will have intentional results from your call-to-actions and other planned activities, and then you will have organic traffic. People talk and share information, so if new folks come across your promotion and reach out to you, you'll want to track that increase in outreach.

Responses and replies to your emails. If you are sending out emails and asking people to personally respond to you with questions, you want to see how effective that strategy is.

Replies to your social media stories. If you are incorporating Facebook or Instagram stories into your campaign, people may respond, so you want to keep tabs on that. Track the type of story—such as Questions, Polls, or Behind the Scenes—that you received responses to as well.

Comments on social media posts, live streams, videos,

and published articles. When you post something or go live, you want to capture any comments or responses. Yes you can see what's working for you, and you can also follow up with each of the people with some information about your offer. Never miss an opportunity to engage.

Responses to direct pitches. If you pitched to media or other companies for business opportunities, you should track who responded and who didn't.

Meetings, calls, and consultations booked. If your lead generation strategy is to book 1:1 meetings, calls, or consults, keep record of everyone who follows through and makes an appointment with you.

Meetings and calls conducted. Just because people book a meeting or call, doesn't mean they will follow through and show up. You hope that people come through, and the majority of them likely will. But you will have some flakes, and that's okay.

Conversions from ads. Ads cost money, so you definitely want to know how your ads are performing. This is something you want to keep an eye on consistently, as you may want to adjust your ad prior to the end of your launch if it's not yielding the results you expected.

Number of events attended. You may have a list of events that you plan to attend to network, speak, or vend. Track how many you made it to and the results. Did people fill out your Jotform? How many Rip cards did you collect? These are all important metrics.

New email subscribers. You should know how big your email list is before your launch so you can track your growth afterwards.

Email unsubscribes. Remember, we're out of our feelings, right? If people leave your list in droves, it could be that your message isn't resonating with people. Or maybe they are not interested in your content at the moment. That is good information to know so you can adjust accordingly.

Sales from brand partners, affiliates, and referrals. If you have strategic partners, you should have links, codes, or some mechanism to track the traffic that comes from each source.

MASTERING SALES

You came here to sell something—a product, a service, a community, an idea, something. So sales is a skillset you have to learn and master.

I know a thing or two about getting people to buy something or buy into something. You name it, I've sold it. I've sold electronics in retail, graphic design service, photography, juices, the list goes on and on.

What I've learned over the years is that the product or service really doesn't matter. If you can sell one thing, you can usually sell any and everything. As long as you believe in it—and yourself.

That is what business is about. Selling yourself. At the end of the day, people are buying you. Your offer is just an extension of who you are and what you can do.

To become good at sales, you have to come out of the shadows. You have to accept that you have to sell and promote yourself. To be honest, if you are unwilling to embrace this, it's going to be next to impossible for you to build a business that's successful.

Once you make that mindset shift, you will be able to sell your butt off. I don't care if you are selling Saltine crackers or six-figure wedding planning packages, these strategies will help you get to the money:

Know yourself. You don't have to become a completely different person to sell. But you do have to find the technique that works best for you. There is no need to be paralyzed by fear because you don't like to speak in front of large crowds, when you can just write great sales copy for your pages and emails and go sell. There are way too many options available to you. Choose the strategy that you can get comfortable with and get to it.

Know your product. You should know your product inside out, upside down, and sideways. Every detail, every feature, the weight, inches, if it turns into a Gremlin when it gets wet...you catch my drift. Consumers can smell inexperience, and it's a huge turnoff. If you get in front of someone who is ready to buy, but you cannot answer their questions properly, you will probably lose that sale.

Know your customer. Everyone has preferences, and you have to know your customers. Do your ideal customers prefer 1:1 calls, or do they prefer to buy right from a page? Are they techies? Do they spend a lot of time on social media, or do they not even know how to post a selfie? Do they spend money? Get into your people so you can know who is for you, and who isn't. Everybody is not a fit for your offer, and that is cool. You only want to invest in the people who are likely to invest in you.

Also, you need to know where your customer is on their journey and where you fit in. If you are a fitness instructor and a man comes into your gym with a goal of becoming a professional bodybuilder, but he can't lift a Cheerio, as the expert, you want to educate him on what it realistically take to get there. If you have a program that could get him to where he wants to be, this is where you would gauge how committed he is by asking the right questions. Is he ready to make the sacrifices necessary? Is he ready to invest $10,000 in your private training program? You need to be clear on where your customer is so you can assess how to handle the sale.

Know the options and trends in your industry. Your customers are making buying decisions based on a number of factors, including what else is out there. So you need to know what's going on in the marketplace. What businesses and offers are available to your potential customers is information you should be aware of. You need to know what other products, services, and communities may be more convenient and more appealing based on their preferences and needs.

Why would a twenty-year old want to pay you to bring Blu-ray DVDs to their house when they can watch Netflix? With awareness of what else exists, you can tailor your offer to better position in the market.

Know how to handle objections. Price, perception of better quality, more convenience. These are all reasons that will make people question if the business next door is better for them. And some people will be vocal about it and let you know. It's tempting to get defensive and show them the door, but there's a better response. *Listening.* You'll show up as the professional you are, and you may actually get some insight on how to refine your product or process based on what else is out there.

Also don't forget, it ain't over 'til it's over. Consumers like to shop around. They very well may loop back. Keep your cool, share value, and encourage people to make the best decision for them. For every one person who doesn't buy, there will be two who will.

Know how to collaborate with your client in the buying decision. People will have questions—a lot of them. So be patient and prepared to answer them. You can put up FAQs on your website. You can get on a follow-up call after the initial consult, if your customer still wants to talk through some things. You can set up a chat bot so you don't have to actually get on the phone. Put some tools in place to help people to make a decision and be willing to support them.

Know how to take your time. Nobody likes to be rushed and pressured into a sale. I am sure you've come across some Slick Sam Salesperson at some point who does everything he can to push you into buying something. He's standing over your shoulder in the store, practically stepping on the back of your shoes while you look around. You're thinking to yourself, *"Whoa, back up, bro!"* We've all been there, and we all hate it. That approach feels desperate and, let's be honest, shady.

You may be excited about your offer and the possibility of the sale, but let people breathe please. Slow down, take your time, listen, and answer questions that your potential clients have. Take cues from them and don't be too pushy.

And a few bonus tips:

Have some swag. Confidence people, confidence. No one will believe in your business more than you. If you are doubting yourself, people will sense that and be hesitant to buy from you. Don't give anyone a reason to second guess you. Own your skills, your results, and what you can do for them.

Walk your customer through the buying process and what happens next. Leave no stone unturned when it comes to the details of your sales process. This goes back to helping your customers to make a buying decision. Your customers should not be wondering what happens after they swipe their credit card. If their product will arrive at their door on a silver platter, carried by a white-gloved waiter, tell them that. Tell them about all the emails they can expect throughout the process, the meeting schedule, the mile-stones. Lay it all out.

Wow them. Let people know how much you love them and that you appreciate the sale. You don't want people to feel like they are just a dollar sign to you. Customer service and appreciation goes a long way. Remind people that they matter.

Take Action

Before you move on to the next chapter, do this:

- Get your mind right in preparation for your launch. Do whatever you need to do to put yourself in a positive place, stay focused, and keep your excitement at an all-time high.

- Double check the "Why Launches Flop" list and make sure you aren't making any of these mistakes to set yourself up for an unsuccessful launch.

- List all the metrics associated with your launch so you can track them.

- Get your sales confidence up.

- Decide how you want to sell, how you'll handle a sales conversation with a potential client or customer, including any objections they may have so you are prepared to answer them.

- Be prepared to see the sale all the way through. Be ready to answer any questions people have, explain your process or product inside out, and make them feel special once they sign on the dotted line.

"You are a dope creator. A genius. An entrepreneur who was willing to try something that has never been done before."

- Audria Richmond

CHAPTER NINE
MASTERING YOUR CLIENTS AND CUSTOMERS

I know it seems odd to talk about customer service in a marketing book, but to me, it's a very necessary component of your marketing—especially for an UnCloned Campaign.

It kills me to see business owners do so much hard work to get the sale, and then drop the ball when servicing the client. It's an area that many small businesses struggle with, and one that can be the most detrimental to your company.

If your service starts to fall apart as soon as a customer pays you, you can practically kiss them goodbye. They may not demand a refund—which does happen—but losing what could have been repeat business or, worse, having someone in the streets badmouthing your company, can actually cost more than the sale itself in the long run. Some say these experiences are bound to happen in business, and that's true to an extent. There will be people you simply cannot please. You can do everything right, dot every "I" and cross every "T", and still not make a customer happy. But those are situations that are beyond your control. You can absolutely control delivering quality service. In fact, let's take it to an UnCloned level:

You can deliver blow-your-damn-mind-every time service. So you should.

I want you to begin to think of your entire client experience as a part of the launch and sales process. You shouldn't stop at launching your offer and getting the sale. Yes, it takes a lot of work just to get to that point. But any successful business owner knows the sale is actually just the beginning of the work. You've got them—now you have to keep them. You are still selling, even once you've bought the customer in, so always keep that in mind.

Another reason why you want to give your customer an amazing experience is referrals. People talk when they have a bad experience, and they do the same when they have a good one.

Since first impressions are lasting impressions, let's focus on onboarding—the process you put in place to bring a client or customer into your company. It doesn't matter if you sell a product or service, you still need an onboarding process that wows your clients and makes them happy they purchased something from you. Their experience with you will go a long way in how they view your company. Wow them and you not only have a happy client, but you have a client who is well positioned to purchase the next product or service from you. Customers that have a great experience are almost guaranteed to buy again and again.

Here's how to onboard your clients like a pro:

Welcome and confirmation. Once your customer makes their payment, they immediately receive a payment confirmation and a warm, welcome email. The email should clearly lay out their next steps and what they need to do.

Send a thank-you note. Another nice touch in the onboarding process is a thank-you note. Reassure your customer they made the best decision by purchasing from you. Bonus points if it's handwritten.

Follow-through and follow-up. If your customer is lagging in getting information back to you to keep their project moving, like a questionnaire, reach out to them. As the product or service provider, it is your responsibility to manage the client. Help them along when you need to. Nurture and support your customers. Don't leave people behind after they've paid you. Let people know you care.

Send something unexpected. Think of ways you can delight your customer. Everyone loves getting gifts in the mail, and they will gush about it all over social media about it. Did someone say free promotion? Find ways to get your customers giddy before, during, and after the sale. Gift them something at multiple touchpoints during their experience with you.

THE POWER OF THE UPSELL

When a customer has had a wow-worthy experience with you, you have a shot to sell into your next product or service. If you don't take it, you're leaving a lot of money on the table. One of the biggest expenses in business is the cost of acquiring a new customer. As a business owner, you can significantly reduce those costs by keeping the clients you have and showing them ways to spend more money with you.

You should have a list of additional products and services ready to offer to every client. If you don't, here are my top five upsell recommendations:

Additional support. How can you help your customer next? Once they get to the end of the road with you, what is the next phase for them in the success journey, and how can you be there to support them? These are opportunities for additional paid products and services.

Companion products and services. What fries can you sell to go with that shake? What do you have that complements their experience and what they just bought from you? Take a second to think through everything your customer could need as it relates to what you do. What tools do they need? Can you create them and add them to your product suite?

VIP experiences, events, and retreats. Live experiences are the perfect upsell to online communities, courses, and programs. When people bond online, they appreciate an opportunity to put faces to names, and to go deeper with what you teach.

Discounts with brand partners. People love perks. If rolling with you means there are benefits, people will gladly buy. Put a package together of all the tools, resources, and services you recommend, negotiate discounts with those companies, and sell the bundle to your clients.

Access to new upcoming products and services. Sneak peeks and exclusivity are always hot-ticket items. Your existing customers want to be first in line to get what's next, so be in position to take advantage of that. If you know what you are launching a few months down the road, share that service at the early-bird, get-it-before-everybody-else-does price.

Take Action

Before you move on to the next chapter, do this:

- Decide how you can make your onboarding process Un-Cloned and epic. This is your opportunity to really make a lasting impression on a client or customer.

- Be ready to upsell people into something else in your product or service suite. Build your list of offers to pitch.

"Wow them and you not only have a happy client, but you have a client who is well positioned to purchase the next product or service from you."

- Audria Richmond

CHAPTER TEN

YOUR UNCLONED MARKETING CAMPAIGN SUCCESS PATH FAST TRACK

Okay, so you want to get right to it? I got you.

If you don't have time to read this entire book from cover to cover, even though I highly recommend that you do, I feel you. I am not a fan of shortcuts in business, but I know you have people to reach and money to make. So I took the highlights from this book and condensed them into this fluff-free, master checklist. Use this list as your blueprint for building your UnCloned Marketing Campaign.

Step One: Establish Your Authority and Credibility (Why Should I Buy From You?)

Your potential clients and customers are looking to buy from one group of people—experts. So you need to show them that you are one. People are expecting you to prove why you are the best choice, and your marketing campaign should do the talking.

1. Gather the proof that demonstrates you are the 'ish. That could be any of the following:

   - **Personal Results.** Be your own testimonial. Whatever it is you sell, you should be your own best customer. Tell your story and how your thing worked for you.

   - **Before and Afters.** When you can show visually how you were able to take someone from Point A to Point B—or maybe even Point Z—your potential customer can begin to imagine themselves experiencing a similar result.

   - **Case Studies.** Give a detailed account of your customer's challenges before they came to you and how you solved their problem with your product or service.

- **Reviews and Testimonials.** Let the world speak for you. If a client brags about you, you want to leverage it to boost your authority and credibility in the market.

2. If you don't have enough proof to support what you offer, now is time to go get it. Dig deeper into your field or industry, build a platform, or strike up a strategic collaboration to leverage someone else's audience.

3. Master your marketing message. Come up with a concise, compelling message to explain what your service or product is and the result it creates.

Step Two: Create Your Free and Paid Offers (What You Sell)

Your offer is what you are giving away or selling.

1. Choose a free offer to give away to potential clients so they can test drive what you do before buying something.

2. Choose a paid offer so your people have something to jump into after you've wowed them with your free offer.

3. UnClone it. Brainstorm on ways to make your offer(s) different from anything people have seen before. Think of how you can uniquely position your offer in the marketplace to make it distinct.

Here is a list of options for your free and paid offers:

- 1-on-1 Calls

- LIVEStreams

- Online and Offline Workshops

- Challenges

- Video Series

- Webinars

- Meetups

- Memberships

- Audits and Assessments

- Audiobooks

- Print Books and Workbooks

- Done for You Resources

- Newsletters

- Magazines

- Software Tools

- Coupons/Discount Codes

- Trial Offers

- Virtual/Live Events and Conferences

- Speaking

- Audio Series/Course

- Podcast/Podcast Series

- Physical and Digital Templates

- VIP Day/Weeks/Weekends

- Masterminds

- Streaming Services

- Products (such as courses, food, beauty products, electronics)

Step Three: Generate Leads (Getting People to See What You're Selling)

This step is all about visibility and driving traffic to your offer(s). When it's time to get eyeballs on your thing, here's what you need to do:

1. Decide if you will use inbound or outbound marketing strategies for your campaign.

    Inbound Lead Strategy Options

    - Social Media (This could be paid traffic, such as ads or sponsored posts, on Facebook, Instagram, Google, or any other platform that offers advertisements.)

    - Social Media Partnerships (This could be streaming from someone else's platform, such as a private Facebook group.)

- Media, Press, and Public Relations

- Affiliate Partners

- Brand Ambassadors

- Live Streaming

- Speaking

- Vending at Local Events

- Your existing clients

   Outbound Lead Generation Strategy Options

- Direct Mail

- Email Marketing

- Direct Email

- Invite-only events

2. If tech is not really your thing, consider one of the follow
   ing lead generation strategies:

- Social Selling. Reach out to potential customers or
  clients via DM. To leverage them to easily skyrocket
  your sales, send a direct message to leads with a cute
  photo—say of you or you working side-by-side with
  a client—or a great introductory video along with a
  request to DM you back to continue the conversation, a
  phone number to reach you for a consultation, via call
  or text or a link to a checkout page to purchase your
  offer or a link to your website to learn more about your

products or services.

- 1-on-1 Calls

- Meetups

- Audits and Assessments

- Networking and Speaking with Lead Capturing Systems (such as Jotforms and Rip Cards)

3. If you want to go high-tech with your campaign, here are some possibilities to consider:

- Challenges

- Video Series

- Webinars

- Events

- Partnerships and Collaborations

- Evergreen Funnels

- Virtual Conferences

- Virtual Breakout Sessions at Events

Step Four: The Marketing Plan (Your Money-Making Game Plan)

Your marketing plan is your playbook that details everything that needs to happen to make your campaign successful.

1. First, write out your marketing plan. Here are the **20 Things Every Marketing Plan should include:**

   - **Purpose of Your Campaign.** You want to be clear on the intent and inspiration behind your campaign. Why are you launching or relaunching this offer? Are you seeking to get new clients and customers? Are you seeking to build your authority and credibility? If you are running a nonprofit, are you setting out to increase volunteers or to make a difference in your community in a big way? Know what your campaign is about and what you are here to do with it.

   - **Your Idea.** What is your idea or concept? For example, when I created the UnCloned Marketing Membership, I wanted a community for business owners to learn proven marketing strategies that increased their profitability. Once I was clear on my idea, I could move into the details of what that would look like. You want to flesh out your idea and be certain that it makes sense for the market.

   - **Your Mission, Vision, and Why.** Next, you'll want to define your mission, vision, and why. You've thought about your purpose, but go deeper and detail your vision for impacting your audience and why it's important to you and them.

   - **What Success Would Look Like for You.** If you could waive a marketing magic wand and have the most successful campaign ever, what would that look like for you? Would it be to make money? Would it be to have new people subscribe to your newsletter? Are you looking to step up your authority and credibility factor in your industry? These are the types of results you are looking for. List them out and include them in your plan.

- **Goals and Objectives.** Keep going with your key goals and objectives. How will you know that your campaign is successful? How much money will you have made or how many new followers will you have? Get specific so you know what results you are looking for.

- **Target Audience/Target Situation™.** If you have an established business, and this is not your first time launching this offer, you want to document who your target audience is. But if this is your first time giving this a try, you may not know exactly who your audience is, but you may know the situation they are struggling with and how your product or services is a fix for their issue. That is your target situation. You want to document which of the two is the focus for your particular campaign.

- **How You Plan to Test Your Idea and Market Research.** In this section of your plan, you want to document the process you will use to determine if the market wants what you offer, before you jump into a full-blown, time consuming marketing campaign. How will you beta test your offer and see if it piques some interest first?

- **Type of Paid Offer.** Are you launching a product, service, event, or a combination of all of these?

- **Details and Summary of Your Paid Offer.** This is where you get into the specifics of your offer.

  If you were explaining your offer to your customer, what would you tell them? What would you include in the product description for a catalog or your sales page? Write everything the offer includes, what the features and benefits are, and the value each of those provides. Anticipate every question your customer may ask about your product or service, and answer them here.

- **How You Plan to Wow and Onboard Your New Clients.** This is the detailed process that lays out what happens once someone decides to take the action you want them to take. Do they receive a welcome email or gift? Are you calling each person to thank them?

- **Type of Free Offer (AKA Lead Magnet).** Write out the details of your free offer. What is it? What does it include? How will people access it?

- **Traffic and Promotion Strategy.** Go back to your notes on your lead generation strategy. Document how you will be driving traffic to your free offer. What process will you use to convert leads from your free offer to your paid offer, or the next step you want them to take, like signing up for a group or coming out to be a part of a fundraising walk or run? If you are running ads, include that. If you are planning to livestream 10 times in a week, include that too. Have a plan for every platform you intend to promote on.

- **Launch Dates and Other Very Important Dates.** This section will be your master calendar and schedule. In addition to the date you will officially launch your offer, you want to document your other key dates as well. Those dates could include when you will need to have each of your promotions designed and ready to go, when your videos will be recorded, or meetings with your launch team. Put all your dates in one place so you have them at a glance.

- **Snapshot and Audit of Your Numbers Before the Launch.** Know your numbers so you have some data and metrics to compare at the end of your launch. How many social media followers did you have? How many subscribers did you have on your newsletter or podcast? How many products had you sold this time last year? With this type of information, you'll be able to better analyze your campaign to determine if it was effective or not.

- **List of Top Promotional Activities.** This is the fun part. Decide what you will be giving away to promote your offer. Are you printing special t-shirts for you and your team? Mailing your attendees branded popcorn to munch on while watching your video series? Giving out discounts for a limited-collection bracelet sold at your boutique? Think about all the creative ways to get the word out about your launch.

- **Assets for Each Phase of the Launch.** Plan out all the assets you'll need for your launch. Think about this in terms of phases and what you need for each one. If you are recording a promotional video, you may need a slide deck and the actual video. For your free offer, you'll probably have some sort of web page for people to opt-in and download the freebie, so you need the page and the freebie too. You may need a special shop for your products if you are selling them online, or new signage for your store if you have a brick-and-mortar location. So you want to detail out everything you need to completely execute your campaign.

- **Production Team and Budget Needed.** If you plan to hire people to help you with your campaign, list out the roles you'd like to hire for. I'll talk about who you should consider for your launch team later in this chapter.

  Know your numbers when it comes to money. You don't want to be in a situation where you are halfway through your launch, and you get hit with some unexpected cost. You should have a budget sheet and a line item for every expense associated with your launch.

- **Schedule of Dates for All Promotional Activities.** Honing in on your promotional phase, list out all of the dates for your activities. When are you mailing out gifts or coupons?

- **How You Plan to Track All Sales.** You have to track

your sales so you know what's coming in. You can use an Excel spreadsheet or some other tool. Or you can check out my sales tracker to make it simple for you **https://audriarichmond.shop/.**

- **How You Plan to Track All Launch Activities.** This is where you track every activity of your launch, including the date you will release it and metrics for success. For example, if I am hosting a virtual conference and giving every person who registers a link to download a digital badge with their picture on it so they can share it on social, I'll want to list that activity out and how I will know how effective that strategy was. I may be tracking shares or downloads from my site. This is the type of information you want to capture here.

2. Get creative with your assets and branding for your campaign. If you need to hire a designer to help, now is the time to hire one. Here's a list of creative that you may need:

   - Logo

   - Packaging or Product Branding

   - Print or social media flyers

   - Countdown Graphics to post on social media leading up to your launch

   - Livestream graphic (This displays while people are waiting for your livestream to start.)

   - Instagram Story Graphics

- Facebook Story Graphics

- Cover for Your Facebook Business Page

- Badges (These are cool for virtual events or challenges; everyone who registers for the event or signs up for the challenge can get one to share on social and drum up promotion for your campaign.)

- Ad graphics

- Email headers

- Workbooks, Checklists, or other templates to support your offer

- Custom Slide Decks

3. And speaking of hiring, this is where you decide if you'll need a launch team. Aside from a designer, you may also want to consider the following service providers to take your launch to the next level:

   - Photographer

   - Videographer

   - Graphic and Website Designer

   - Copywriter

   - Social Media Pro/Specialist

   - Tech and Marketing Automation Pro

Step Five: Launching and Sales (It's Time to Make Some Money)

Let's launch!

1. Prepare your mindset and your energy for your launch. You want everything around you as positive as possible.

2. Determine which metrics you need to track once you launch your campaign. You want to know your numbers, which, depending on your campaign, can include:

    Metrics for your specific business. Depending on what your offer is, you'll want to track related metrics. So if you were selling a new toothbrush in your dental clinic, you'll be measuring the number of brushes sold. If you have a membership, then you are tracking new members, and so on.

    Daily sales from your products and services. Stay on top of your money. You want to look at your sales reports at least once a day.

    Social media growth and increase in followers, likes, etc. Know where you start before your campaign begins. Your marketing plan should include your numbers for all your social media platforms, and you want to track growth throughout your launch.

    Call-to-Action responses. Pay attention to what you're asking people to do and if they are taking action. If at the end of your posts, you are asking people to click a link to take them to your registration page, you want to track those clicks.

Number of direct messages and social media comments and conversations. You will have intentional results from your call-to-actions and other planned activities, and then you will have organic traffic. People talk and share information, so if new folks come across your promotion and reach out to you, you'll want to track that increase in outreach.

Responses and replies to your emails. If you are sending out emails and asking people to personally respond to you with questions, you want to see how effective that strategy is.

Replies to your social media stories. If you are incorporating Facebook or Instagram stories into your campaign, people may respond, so you want to keep tabs on that. Track the type of story—such as Questions, Polls, or Behind the Scenes—that you received responses to as well.

Comments on social media posts, live streams, videos and published articles. When you post something or go live, you want to capture any comments or responses. Yes you can see what's working for you, and you can also follow up with each of the people with some information about your offer. Never miss an opportunity to engage.

Responses to direct pitches. If you pitched to media or other companies for business opportunities, you should track who responded and who didn't.

Meetings, calls, and consultations booked. If your

lead generation strategy is to book 1:1 meetings, calls, or consults, keep record of everyone who follows through and makes an appointment with you.

Meetings and calls conducted. Just because people book a meeting or call, doesn't mean they will follow through and show up. You hope that people come through, and the majority of them likely will. But you will have some flakes, and that's okay.

Conversions from ads: Ads cost money, so you definitely want to know how your ads are performing. This is something you want to keep an eye on consistently, as you may want to adjust your ad prior to the end of your launch if it's not yielding the results you expected.

Number of events attended. You may have a list of events that you plan to attend to network, speak, or vend. Track how many you made it to and the results. Did people fill out your JotForm? How many Rip cards did you collect? These are all important metrics.

New email subscribers. You should know how big your email list is before your launch, so you can track your growth afterwards.

Email unsubscribes. Remember, we're out of our feelings, right? If people leave your list in droves, it could be that your message isn't resonating with people. Or maybe they are not interested in your content at the moment. That is good information to know so you can adjust accordingly.

Sales from brand partners, affiliates, and referrals. If you have strategic partners, you should have links, codes, or some mechanism to track the traffic that comes from each source.

Step Six: Mastering Your Clients and Customers (You Got Them...Now You Gotta Keep Them)

Onboard your customers like a pro. Incorporate special touches like handwritten thank-you notes, gifts, and consistent follow through into your process to keep your customers happy.

When you make your clients happy, they are more than happy to pay you for more services. Take advantage of opportunities to upsell them into additional services such as:

- **Additional support.** How can you help your customer next? Once they get to the end of the road with you, what is the next phase for them in the success journey, and how can you be there to support them? These are opportunities for additional paid products and services.

- **Companion products and services**. What fries can you sell to go with that shake? What do you have that complements their experience and what they just bought from you? Take a second to think through everything your customer could need as it relates to what you do. What tools do they need? Can you create them and add them to your product suite?

- **VIP experiences, events, and retreats.** Live experiences are the perfect upsell to online communities, courses, and programs. When people bond online, they appreciate an opportunity to put faces to names, and to go deeper with what you teach.

- **Discounts with brand partners.** People love perks. If rolling with you means that there are benefits, people will gladly buy. Put a package together of all the tools, resources, and services that you recommend, negotiate discounts with those companies, and sell the bundle to your clients.

- **Access to new upcoming products and services.** Sneak peeks and exclusivity are always hot-ticket items. Your existing customers want to be first in line to get what's next, so be in position to take advantage of that. If you know what you are launching a few months down the road, share that service at the early-bird, get-it-be-fore-everybody-else-does price.

- **Being good at sales is all about knowledge.** You need to know how you like to sell your product and industry inside out, your customer, and your competition and what they're offering. This will help you to be able to effective-ly overcome any objections your potential customers or clients may have.

- **Increase your sales swag.** Be sure you are confident about yourself and your offer, that you answer all your customer's questions—preferably before they can even ask—and wow people with great service and something to show your appreciation.

CONCLUSION

If you are reading this, it means you have officially completed this book and you are ready to go launch an UnCloned Marketing Campaign. Now it's not going to be easy, but you are light years ahead of people who will never truly know what it means to launch a profitable marketing campaign.

I shared my proven framework, the *"UnCloned Marketing Method™"* with you so you know what it takes to launch. The goal of this book is for you to reference it every time you are ready to launch a marketing campaign.

If you would like to deepen your learning and get support when it comes to your marketing, I want to share a few resources below to get you started:

Consulting & Coaching. If you are looking for me to hold you by the hand and support you with ideation, strategizing marketing, or launching, I got you. Just visit my website at **www.audriarichmond.com** to learn more about the services and programs I offer to help you.

Online UnCloned Marketing Shop. In my online marketing shop, I offer tons of tools, resources, checklists, and mini-courses that are designed to help you UnClone your marketing. Here, you will find sales trackers, Canva templates, and so much more. You can shop now at **www.audriarichmond.shop.**

UnCloned Mastery Mastermind. This is for my elite entrepreneurs who don't have time to waste and want to expedite the growth of their business. In this mastermind, I give my clients access to all my done-for-you marketing systems and processes. You have access to ask questions in both group and 1-on-1 settings. We also host fun, live events where you'll get to meet me and the other mastermind members in person to reset throughout the year, receive more hands-on support to ensure that we are moving in the right direction. If you would like to learn more, please visit **www.audriarichmond.com** to apply now.

You can also find me online via your favorite social media platform via the links below.

https://www.facebook.com/audriadrichmond/

https://www.instagram.com/audriarichmond/

https://twitter.com/audriarichmond

https://www.youtube.com/user/audriarichmond

Until we meet again, let's go build an **UNCLONED BRAND!**

Love,

Audria Richmond

ABOUT THE AUTHOR

Born to break ground, Audria Richmond is the Marketing and Launch Strategist you find when you know it's time to scale your business model, automate your marketing, and multiply your money. A visionary whose name will be spoken alongside the most celebrated innovators of her time, Audria has an imagination and a pulse on innovation that keeps her paces ahead of every industry. With her incomparable formula of business strategy, unquenchable creativity, and tech-savviness, Audria is a force that is impossible to reckon with.

An entrepreneur at her core, her hunger for success has built several business ventures from photography to juicing. Each endeavor led Audria closer to the one piece of her profit puzzle that she was missing—marketing mastery. Once she found it, the world was never the same.

Since 2014, her consulting company has earned over $700K in revenue without an expansive team, proving that profitability is always possible as long as a genius is behind the scenes. Now well known for her disruptive take on marketing, Audria has become sought after for her ability to strategically map and implement talked-about marketing campaigns that lead to explosive results.

With one of the most unmatched and intriguing brands ever seen, including her signature *UnCloned Marketing Method*™, Audria is always challenging every marketing rule ever written—and replacing them with her own. A breathing billboard for her trademark tagline, "Be the First to Do It First," her body of work is a passionate manifesto to business owners everywhere to take the risks with their marketing that will lead to the rise in their profitability. Through her bestselling books, first-of-its-kind app, and consulting, Audria has helped thousands of entrepreneurs and companies to stake their claim in the market, moving from doing it like everybody else to completely UnCloned.

She is disruptive. She is brilliant. She is Audria Richmond.

WWW.AUDRIARICHMOND.SHOP

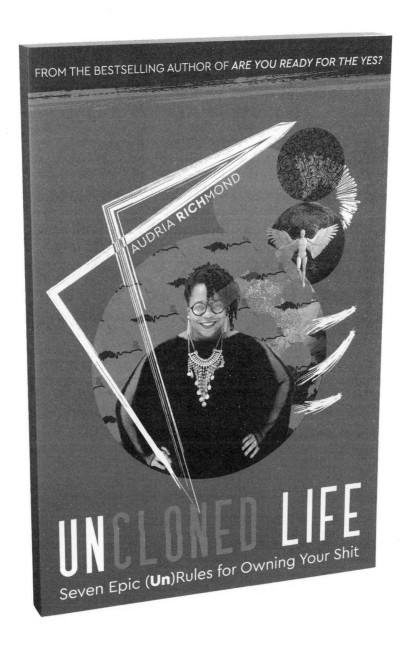

WWW.AUDRIARICHMOND.SHOP

WWW.UNCLONEDTRIBEAPP.COM